Turtle

Animal
Series editor: Jonathan Burt

Already published

Albatross Graham Barwell · *Ant* Charlotte Sleigh · *Ape* John Sorenson · *Badger* Daniel Heath Justice
Bat Tessa Laird · *Bear* Robert E. Bieder · *Beaver* Rachel Poliquin · *Bedbug* Klaus Reinhardt
Bee Claire Preston · *Beetle* Adam Dodd · *Bison* Desmond Morris · *Camel* Robert Irwin
Cat Katharine M. Rogers · *Chicken* Annie Potts · *Cockroach* Marion Copeland · *Cow* Hannah Velten
Crocodile Dan Wylie · *Crow* Boria Sax · *Deer* John Fletcher · *Dog* Susan McHugh · *Dolphin* Alan Rauch
Donkey Jill Bough · *Duck* Victoria de Rijke · *Eagle* Janine Rogers · *Eel* Richard Schweid
Elephant Dan Wylie · *Falcon* Helen Macdonald · *Flamingo* Caitlin R. Kight · *Fly* Steven Connor
Fox Martin Wallen · *Frog* Charlotte Sleigh · *Giraffe* Edgar Williams · *Goat* Joy Hinson
Goldfish Anna Marie Roos · *Gorilla* Ted Gott and Kathryn Weir · *Guinea Pig* Dorothy Yamamoto
Hare Simon Carnell · *Hedgehog* Hugh Warwick · *Hippopotamus* Edgar Williams · *Horse* Elaine Walker
Hyena Mikita Brottman · *Human* Amanda Rees and Charlotte Sleigh · *Jellyfish* Peter Williams
Kangaroo John Simons · *Kingfisher* Ildiko Szabo · *Leech* Robert G. W. Kirk and Neil Pemberton
Leopard Desmond Morris · *Lion* Deirdre Jackson · *Lizard* Boria Sax · *Llama* Helen Cowie
Lobster Richard J. Kin · *Mole* Steve Gronert Ellerhoff · *Monkey* Desmond Morris · *Moose* Kevin Jackson
Mosquito Richard Jones · *Moth* Matthew Gandy · *Mouse* Georgie Carroll · *Octopus* Richard Schweid
Ostrich Edgar Williams · *Otter* Daniel Allen · *Owl* Desmond Morris · *Oyster* Rebecca Stott
Parrot Paul Carter · *Peacock* Christine E. Jackson · *Pelican* Barbara Allen · *Penguin* Stephen Martin
Pig Brett Mizelle · *Pigeon* Barbara Allen · *Polar Bear* Margery Fee · *Rat* Jonathan Burt
Rhinoceros Kelly Enright · *Salmon* Peter Coates · *Sardine* Trevor Day · *Scorpion* Louise M. Pryke
Seal Victoria Dickenson · *Shark* Dean Crawford · *Sheep* Philip Armstrong · *Skunk* Alyce Miller
Snail Peter Williams · *Snake* Drake Stutesman · *Sparrow* Kim Todd · *Spider* Katarzyna and Sergiusz
Michalski · *Squid* Martin Wallen · *Swallow* Angela Turner · *Swan* Peter Young · *Tiger* Susie Green
Tortoise Peter Young · *Trout* James Owen · *Turtle* Louise M. Pryke · *Vulture* Thom van Dooren
Walrus John Miller and Louise Miller · *Wasp* Richard Jones · *Whale* Joe Roman
Wild Boar Dorothy Yamamoto · *Wolf* Garry Marvin · *Woodpecker* Gerard Gorman
Zebra Christopher Plumb and Samuel Shaw

Turtle

Louise M. Pryke

REAKTION BOOKS

For Charlotte, who loves nature

Published by
REAKTION BOOKS LTD
Unit 32, Waterside
44–48 Wharf Road
London N1 7UX, UK
www.reaktionbooks.co.uk

First published 2021
Copyright © Louise M. Pryke 2021

Printed and bound in India by Replika Press Pvt. Ltd

A catalogue record for this book is available from the British Library

ISBN 978 1 78914 336 2

Contents

Introduction:
Swimming in the Slow Lane with Turtles 7

1 A Basic Guide to Turtle Zoology 15

2 Turtles in the Ancient World 43

3 Turtles, Culture and Community 63

4 Turtles, Trade and Technology 81

5 Modern Art and Literature 113

6 Turtle Power: Popular Culture and Turtles 135

7 The Turtle's Tail: The Environment
and the Future 155

Timeline 170
References 173
Bibliography 185
Associations and Websites 187
Acknowledgements 189
Photo Acknowledgements 191
Index 195

Introduction:
Swimming in the
Slow Lane with Turtles

For thousands of years of history, turtles have been linked to the natural environment in human thought. In recent years, the image of a sea turtle unhurriedly swimming through clear marine waters has become a potent symbol for the global conservation movement, highlighting the need for preserving endangered species and their habitats. Yet beneath this passive image lies a sturdy eco-warrior, with a reputation for creativity and wisdom.

Turtles have a distinctive relationship with their environment, inhabiting both terrestrial and aquatic habitats. This flexibility lends a paradoxical element to their image. Many species of turtle are primarily aquatic animals, but most require air to breathe, and lay their eggs on land. In form, turtles are unique: they are 'reptiles', have beaks and wear an armour-like shell that is 'as unlikely as it has been influential'.[1] Their successes are secured by playing the long game: sea turtles can swim and dive for vast distances, and can navigate their voyages using geomagnetism as a kind of internal GPS. With 356 known species, turtles inhabit every continent except Antarctica, and every ocean but the Arctic and Antarctic. For over 100 million years, turtles have played a crucial part in maintaining healthy marine ecosystems, through transporting nutrients from oceans to beach systems.[2]

Ancient and, in some species, long-lived, turtles' seeming lethargy has not precluded them from having a powerful impact on

A green turtle swimming in Hawaiian waters.

7

their natural surroundings, and on human culture. Their images are found in rock art in Australia, as well as in petroglyphs in North America. Turtles are connected to knowledge in the world's earliest literature, with the image of the wise turtle persisting into popular culture of the modern day. Turtles play a complicated and pivotal role in their terrestrial and aquatic environments, and their symbolic role in human thought is equally nuanced.

So, what is a turtle? The word 'turtle' generally describes all animals with a bony shell and a backbone, which may locally be referred to as turtles, tortoises or terrapins.[3] The term 'tortoise' generally describes a land-based turtle, and 'terrapin' refers to more aquatic species, but both tortoises and terrapins can be accurately described as turtles.

The sturdy protection of the shell has made this feature of the animal's physique a popular part of its mythology and dominated the creature's image. Myths from numerous cultures portray turtles using their shelled backs to boost the buoyancy of those around them, holding aloft deities, other animals and even the entire universe. The antiquity of the turtle, and its presence in aquatic and terrestrial environments, has perhaps inspired its appearance in creation myths.

In the present day, turtles continue to display their ancient ties to wisdom in film and television, with the animals depicted as friendly protagonists in artistic works directed at young audiences. The broad appreciation of turtles by children is perhaps somewhat unexpected – turtles are not cuddly animals, and their characteristic slowness means they would never be considered a particularly flashy creature. Yet the steady turtle has an unhurried

Turtle, frontal view.

charisma. Part of the creature's slow-burning magnetism comes from its association with antiquity; some turtles are known for their longevity, and they are among the most ancient animals still existing on earth. The prehistoric quality of turtles may partially explain their appeal to children. The attraction of turtles, tortoises and terrapins for children can further be seen in their popularity as pet animals: a fascination that contributes to their decline.

A sea turtle painted on rock, at Djulirri in northwest Arnhem Land. The site is considered Australia's earliest known example of 'contact art', and turtle shells are thought to have been among the items traded by Indigenous communities with early visitors to the continent.

Turtles are recognizable internationally through their association with the 'heroes in a half-shell' – the Teenage Mutant Ninja
Turtles. Indeed, the image of the turtle as a warrior is common to
many ancient and modern cultural depictions of the creature. The
popularity of the warrior turtle likely has its origins in the observation of its distinctive physical form, with the shell providing a
kind of natural body armour.

The shell of the turtle is a natural wonder. Shells are a multi-pur-
pose accessory for the turtle: as well as shielding the creature from
predators, they provide protection from the natural elements, and
even hold a handy store of minerals. For some tortoises, also, the
defensive use of the shell is accompanied by an offensive one,
used for battling rivals. The diversity of uses for the shell among

A desert tortoise.

Harriet Miller's depiction of a sea turtle on a beach, from Olive Thorne's *Little Folks in Feathers and Fur, and Others in Neither* (1875).

turtles has echoes of its utilization by humans, with turtle shells being used to make rattles and drums, and to create tools for divination in ancient cultures.

To appreciate turtles is to embrace the subtler side of the natural world. Turtles are complicated and diverse animals, who have retained a dignified sense of mystery to their image despite years of human interaction, exploitation and veneration. They are at the forefront of current debates about climate change and global warming because of environmental sex determination in many species. Increasing global temperatures are resulting in a greater gender imbalance among turtle hatchlings, and in some instances, no hatchlings at all. In many ways, turtles have never been so visible to a broad modern audience, but generally, populations continue to decline and even become extinct. We have much to learn about these animals and their complex role in the world's cultural and natural environment. Indeed, developing a greater awareness of turtles is of vital importance for their continued survival.

Drawing of a hawksbill sea turtle, from a history of turtles of the 1790s.

Exploring the intricacy of the turtle, as a cultural symbol and a biological animal, requires an appreciation of the deep

Tab. XVIII. A.

Testudo imbricata Linn.

connection between the creature and its environment. In the increasingly fast-paced world of the twenty-first century, it has never been more important to consider the cultural history of this remarkable animal, and take a swim in the slow lane of life with the turtle.

1 A Basic Guide to Turtle Zoology

Nature does not forget beauty of outline
even in a mud turtle's shell.
Henry David Thoreau

Turtles are among the world's most ancient 'reptiles'. The discovery of turtle fossils from over 200 million years ago means these half-shelled mariners once shared the earth with dinosaurs. The extreme antiquity of the turtle, and its prevalence and diversity in the modern day, shows an animal in possession of a certain biological virtuosity. The turtle is a creature whose physiology spans great extremes, and one that seems at times physically at odds with its environment.

The turtle is an animal which lays eggs on land, yet lives in water, and in this way the turtle's life cycle encompasses both terrestrial and aquatic zones. Both environments are crucial for survival, but the creature's remarkable physiology means it inhabits each zone uniquely. The turtle's graceful glide through the water may be contrasted with its ungainly gait on dry land. While some turtles dive to depths of more than 1,000 m (3,280 ft), all turtles can breathe air. The turtle's seeming tolerance for accommodating extremes is further reflected in its physical shape and behaviours. The creature's tough upper shell, or carapace, provides a protective contrast with its soft body. While universally famed for its slow pace, the turtle can travel for extremely long distances.

Understanding the remarkable and unique aspects of turtle physiology is an area of academic research that, while rapidly

The bones of a prehistoric sea turtle on display at the National Museum of Natural History, Washington, DC.

advancing, remains incomplete. There are many unanswered questions about the anatomy and physiology of turtles, and knowledge of their behaviours and origins is still unfolding. The many unanswered questions enhance the sense of mystery around this ancient animal, and its relationship with the natural environment.

EVOLUTION AND TAXONOMY

Turtles are ancient creatures, belonging to the most ancient line of reptiles which appeared more than 200 million years ago in the late Triassic period.[1] The first sea turtles are thought to have evolved during the Cretaceous period, over 110 million years ago. While turtles were long considered to be reptiles, more recent

Assembled sea turtles, from Ernst Haeckel's *Kunstformen der Natur* (1904).

research has shown the need for a more nuanced perspective on the animals' taxonomy.

Before the nineteenth century, naturalists had largely divided the animal kingdom into two main categories: vertebrates and invertebrates. In 1854 the French zoologist Georges Cuvier broadened the system of classification to four main groups (*embranchements*). In the group called Vertebrata, Cuvier included a class of 'Reptilia'. In this category, Cuvier placed the turtle.[2] Cuvier was particularly intrigued by the shell of the turtle, which he described as a 'double buckler' in which the body was enclosed. The animal's anatomy was regarded by Cuvier as like 'an animal turned inside-out'.

In 1866 the German zoologist Ernst Haeckel observed that turtles, crocodilians, lizards, birds, mammals and snakes are all amniotes, that is, animals with a unique kind of egg, with an embryo surrounded by a fluid-filled sac and amniotic membrane, or ambrion. From that time, the classes of Reptilia and Amphibia became permanently separated. Throughout the twentieth century, the term 'Reptilia' was traditionally defined as encompassing all amniotes except mammals and birds, a classification into which the turtle was comfortably included.

In the twenty-first century, the turtle is no longer easily described as a reptile. The shifting taxonomic focus from adult animals to eggs, through to genes and molecular data, has seen the turtle's classification exploring new ground. Molecular data supports the view of turtles as diapsids, a sister group to archosaurs (a group thought to contain crocodiles, dinosaurs and birds).[3] Diapsids are named for having two holes in each side of their skulls, a feature that developed around 300 million years ago. Synapsids, in contrast, are a class of animals with a single skull opening behind each eye. While 'reptile' may still be applied as part of general vernacular, the scientific discussion surrounding a more accurate definition is by no means settled.[4] It is generally thought that the prehistory of the turtle involved a terrestrial origin. Evidence supporting this view includes the turtle's use of land rather than aquatic areas to lay its eggs, and its taxonomic status as a reptile. Yet the matter remains a topic of scholarly debate.

The world's oldest turtle was long believed to be an extinct animal named *Proganochelys quenstedti,* discovered in 1887 by George Baur. Although not identical to modern turtles, *Proganochelys* greatly resembled later members of its family, including having a shell, the more recent turtle's most distinguishing feature. One way to tell the difference between this ancient species and more recent varieties might have been to open its mouth – unlike modern turtles, *Proganochelys* had teeth. No currently existing turtles have teeth, although hatchling turtles emerge from their eggs using a caruncle, or egg-tooth, and adult turtles use their hard beaks to bite. Turtle enthusiasts from the Renaissance

Another turtle fossil, *Proganochelys quenstedti,* in a German museum.

rijs similis est capite ac testa, sed maior: caput nunquam in testa condit, sed semper exertum habet: ac ceruicem tantùm pro arbitrio modo extendit, modò contrahit, &c. Capta est immanis in mari nostro, anno 1510.quæ bigis utq trahebatur, &c, Rondeletius. ¶ Χελώνη θαλαττία Græcis, et quanquam χέλυς Aristoteli semper Testudinem in dulci aqua significet, Plinius tamen Murem marinum dixit. Et Eustathius: ὁ θαλάσσιος μῦς (inquit) à uulgo perperam ὀρνίθιον (malim cum tenui ὀρνίθιον) uocatur. Nos de uocabulis μῦς, σμῦς, σμῦς, multa protulimus in Commentario nostro De quadrupedibus ouiparis. Mus aquatilis Plinio, testudo lutaria est. Idem Murem marinum modò pro eadem Testudine lutaria, modò pro marina uertit. Legitur & Omys (ὦμυς) apud Aristotelem De partibus 3.9. Omis marina apud Kiranidem legitur, quidam (inquit) ὠμίδια uocant: eò quòd in humeris magnam uim habeat, nam ὦμος est humerus. Inuenitur & Omidium, diminutiuè.

ITAL. HISPAN. GALL. Videmox in secunda specie.
GERM. Ein Meerschilrkrott.

Mus mar.

Omys.

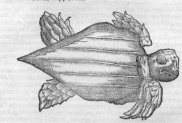

Testudinis (marinæ nimirum)hæc icon Venetijs efficta est: nulli illarum quas Rondeletius exhibet, similis. Dentibus quidem Testudines omnes carere Rondeletius docet: nes suspicer pictoris culpa non rectè dentes huic nostræ attributos. GERM. Ein andere figur einer Meerschilrkrott.

TESTV.

may have been surprised by the absence of teeth in adult turtles due to the influence of the Swiss naturalist Conrad Gessner. His publication *Nomenclator aquatilium animantium* (1560) contained an illustrated turtle based on a woodcut, complete with jagged teeth. Gessner's landmark work, *Historia animalium,* shows the sea turtle with a beak.

The proto-turtle *Proganochelys* was thought the world's most primitive turtle for over a century, until the discovery of an even older turtle, *Odontochelys semitestacea,* in 2008. The fossil turtle's name means 'toothed turtle in a half-shell', reflecting the fact that the extinct creature had a shell covering its belly but not its back. The reign of *Odontochelys* as the most ancient turtle known to science was comparatively brief, ending abruptly when it was usurped by *Pappochelys rosinae,* an extinct turtle found in Germany in 2015.

The new fossil, *Pappochelys,* was named by its discoverers, palaeontologists Rainer Schoch and Hans-Dieter Sues. The name *Pappochelys* comes from the Greek meaning 'grandfather turtle', in a nod to the extreme antiquity of the creature and the importance of the find. *Pappochelys* lived in the Middle Triassic period, around 240 million years ago. The shape of *Pappochelys*' skull has led researchers to argue that the fossil belonged to the taxonomic group of diapsids, an eclectic assembly of animals including crocodiles, snakes and birds.

To put the antiquity of this 'grandfather turtle' into perspective, current dating would place it either just before, or occurring alongside, the appearance of earth's first dinosaurs. The world's oldest known dinosaur was discovered in Tanzania in 2012, and is recognized by the name of *Nyasasaurus parringtoni.* The animal that had previously been thought to be the oldest known dinosaur was an omnivorous creature named *Eoraptor,* which would have appeared on the evolutionary scene shortly after *Pappochelys.*

Conrad Gessner's turtle woodcut, 'testudum marinarum', from his *Nomenclator aquatilium animantium* (1560).

A turtle fossil, a holotype of *Pappochelys rosinae*.

1 cm

In 2018 a new turtle fossil was discovered of the previously unknown species *Eorhynchochelys sinensis* in southwestern China. The new discovery is thought to be the remains of an animal that lived around 230 million years ago, and provides an evolutionary link between *Pappochelys* and *Odontochelys*. This turtle, whose name means 'dawn beak turtle from China', had a beak but no shell, and was around 2 m (6½ ft) in length. The recent discoveries of prehistoric turtles have given important clues about the animal's evolution, yet there is still a great deal about turtles and their origins which remains to be known.

The shell of the turtle dominates its image, but there was a time (admittedly a very long time ago) when it seems turtles did not have shells. Modern turtles likely have a distant relative in *Eunotosaurus*, an extinct reptile from the Permian period. The shell has long been thought of as a defensive adaptation, but a 2016 study discovered proto-turtles likely developed shells to help with burrowing, some 250 million years ago.[5] The development of the shell in stem turtles (early creatures closely related to turtles, but not scientifically defined as turtles) may have assisted in their transition from terrestrial to aquatic environments.[6] Although present-day desert tortoises (*Gopherus agassizii*) may at times use the front edge of the shell to assist with pushing material out of their burrows, like other modern turtles, they use their powerful forelimbs, rather than their shells, for digging.

The top of the turtle's shell is called the carapace, and the bottom is called the plastron. In most turtles these two plates are locked together on the sides by a supportive structure called a bridge. The outer surface of the shell is generally covered by plates called scutes, which are made of keratin and more or less consistent across most species of turtle. The shell is a living part of the turtle; it has blood and a nerve supply, and is capable of growing and changing. Turtle shells show a great deal of diversity between species, with some turtles having a more obviously bony shell, and others, such as the leatherback sea turtle, having a thick, oily skin covering their carapace.

A turtle's shell is a marvel of multifunctionality. The soft body and vital organs of the turtle are protected by the shell's hard

Eastern box turtle in Florida.

outer surfaces. The head and other appendages can also be drawn inwards for protection by the shell, and some turtles, such as the box turtle, can use a hinged section of the lower shell to seal themselves completely inside an impregnable 'box'. Sea turtles, on the other hand, have a flatter shell and flippers to help them glide swiftly through the ocean. Both adaptations make it impossible for the sea turtle to draw its appendages into its shell. For land-based and aquatic turtles, the shell may also provide further protection through a camouflaging effect.

As well as providing defence from predators and protection from potential crush injuries, the turtle's shell can at times be used offensively. Male tortoises may use the thickened edges of their lower shells as a ramming weapon. Some species of turtle have developed the edges of their lower shells into a type of natural hook. This hook can be used for flipping over a rival; assisting in the process of digging; or even inflicting a goring injury, almost in the style of a horn.

A green turtle blends in with its surroundings (Green Island, off the coast of Queensland).

The shell protects the turtle from the elements, and provides it with a major store of minerals. This reserve can be used for regulating mineral levels, and adapting to environmental circumstances. Turtles who are submerged under water for long periods can release minerals to regulate the pH levels of their blood and bodily fluids. In western painted turtles (*Chrysemys picta bellii*), this ability allows the animals to survive in an environment without air for over 170 days, longer than any other tetrapod (four-legged vertebrate). Pregnant turtles also release specific minerals from their shells – calcium and phosphate – to send to their oviducts, for use in making eggshells for their babies.

There is great diversity among the hundreds of turtle species, in terms of size, behaviours and geographical range. The smallest turtles, such as the common musk turtle (or 'stinkpot'), may grow to just 5 cm (2 in.) in length, while the largest in the group is the leatherback sea turtle, which can weigh more than 900 kg

Leatherback sea turtle (*Dermochelys coriacea*) in the U.S. Virgin Islands National Park.

(2,000 lb). Some extinct species of turtle, such as those in the genera *Archelon*, were even larger, weighing over 2,000 kg (4,400 lb).

Turtles, like many reptiles, are vertebrate tetrapods, meaning they have four limbs. For aquatic turtles, these limbs take the form of flippers for swimming, while land-based turtles (or tortoises) have legs more suitable for navigating terrestrial environments. Turtles are ectotherms, meaning that, like reptiles, their body temperature is greatly determined by external conditions, rather than being largely regulated by internal or metabolic processes. Despite their status as ectotherms, some species of turtle have an excellent ability to regulate their own body temperature, or 'thermoregulate'. Leatherback turtles can keep a temperature of 25°C (77°F) while swimming through waters that are cooler by almost 20°C. This ability allows leatherbacks to swim through tropical waters without overheating, and navigate ice floes without freezing.

The turtle's shape and behaviour reflect a compromise between inhabiting the depths of aquatic environments and moving efficiently on land. Marine turtles may only spend fractions of their lives on land, yet this time is of crucial importance to the continuation of their gene pool, and so holds a 'strong selective pressure'.[7]

A further area of compromise is necessitated by the marine turtle's ancient origins. The animal's adaptations to ocean and terrestrial environments are built around the biological reality of the turtle's basic body plan, which involves a sturdy, somewhat inflexible shell – at times referred to as 'the armoured tank'. The shell of the sea turtle is largely responsible for its remarkable and distinctive motion. The rigidity of the animal's tough shell gives it little room to move, which might lead to the expectation of an awkward and ungainly swimmer. On the contrary, however, the turtle excels in the water both in terms of its powerful swimming ability and the gracefulness of its motions.

While the sea turtle's flippers are primarily used for propelling it through water, recent research has shown the surprising adaptability of the sea turtle's limbs. Turtle flippers can be used to manipulate prey, despite being evolutionarily designed for locomotion.[8] Turtles can use their flippers for a variety of tasks, such as rolling a scallop on the sea floor, tossing their prey into the air to stun it, or even striking the prey in a chopping action. The ability of turtles to 'karate-chop' prey made international headlines, and drew comparisons with famous chelonian martial artists the Teenage Mutant Ninja Turtles.[9] The use of limbs for foraging has also been observed in several species of terrestrial or semi-aquatic turtles. The use of flippers for finding food both in land- and water-dwelling turtles suggests the behaviour may have been present in an ancestral turtle.

TURTLE LIFE CYCLE

Turtles and tortoises share many features of their life cycle. They are all hatched from eggs, are relatively slow to reach sexual maturity and live for long periods of time. Alongside this similarity, there is great variety in the life cycles of different turtles.

Turtles and tortoises begin their lives in eggs. In marine turtles, these eggs typically occupy nests on beaches, and for river turtles the eggs may be found on sandbanks. All turtles and tortoises lay their eggs on land, with one exception – the northern snake-necked turtle (*Macrochelodina rugosa*) from Australia.

The Australian northern snake-necked turtles are found in the waterways of Australia and southern New Guinea, and they are known for their strongly aquatic behaviour. They tend to walk along the bottom of waterways rather than swimming, and make their homes in freshwater rivers, lakes and swamps with sandy or muddy bottoms. The Australian northern snake-necked turtle has been described as an 'aquatic vacuum cleaner', feeding on fish, amphibians and other invertebrates.[10] The comparison with a vacuum cleaner may seem unflattering, suggestive of a lack of discernment, but it is an apt description in terms of the turtle's behaviour in hunting for food. The long-necked turtle lies in wait for prey, squeezing between rocks and logs or burying itself in mud. The eponymous neck of the animal is tucked in close to its body. Once suitable prey comes into range, the turtle lunges its head and neck forwards, opening its mouth and throat to create a vacuum, dragging water and the prey into its mouth.

Indigenous Australians long held traditional knowledge of the egg-laying behaviour of the snake-necked turtle. It was only as recently as the 1980s that this awareness spread to the international scientific community. An Australian biologist, Rod Kennett, was studying the nesting behaviour of turtles in Australia's Northern Territory. Through consultation with traditional landowners in the area, Kennett developed an understanding of the distinctive egg-laying behaviour of the long-necked turtle. Using radiotelemetry, Kennett located the nesting sites of the turtles underwater by placing transmitters inside pregnant female long-necked turtles. When the turtle's eggs were laid, Kennett traced the location of the nests, finding that they were indeed underwater.

In circumnavigating the obstacles to reproduction caused by extremes of weather, the northern long-necked turtle risks a further biological impediment. Most turtle eggs will perish if placed in water. Usually, water would be drawn through the shell of a submerged egg, through the pressure of osmotic potential. The egg would then expand and crack, destroying the embryo. Eggs of northern long-necked turtles have an unusually thick and hydrophobic membrane surrounding the yolk, which protects the embryo. This allows the eggs to stay safely submerged for long periods of time. This is considered an adaptive response to the natural extremes of the Australian environment. In the areas inhabited by the turtle, immense wet seasons occur frequently yet unpredictably, and dramatically change the terrain and water levels. The problem of inhospitable nesting sites is found in other species – the common snapping turtle may trek up to 5 km (3 mi.) in search of a suitable location to lay her eggs.

Following their migration to the water, marine turtle hatchlings spend their early years in the open ocean, before returning as juveniles to coastal waters. The period between hatching and reaching a juvenile age may be as long as ten years. The activities of the young turtle out in the open ocean during this time are extremely poorly understood – it was referred to by legendary turtle expert Archie Carr as the turtle's 'lost years'.

As juveniles, marine turtles forage in coastal areas, and the animals show great mobility in this period of their lives. Between ten and fifteen years after hatching, or much longer in some species, turtles reach sexual maturity and begin to mate and reproduce. Turtles can successfully reproduce for most of their lives, although there is some suggestion that the quality of eggs from female turtles might experience some decline late in life.

Mating sea turtles in the Ambracian Gulf, Greece.

Turtles are not known for their social interactivity. This seemingly asocial quality has been anthropomorphically interpreted as shyness, and is referenced in expressions such as 'coming out of one's shell'. Yet turtles have intriguing sex lives, filled with danger and sensuous flourishes. Head bobbing and facial stroking form part of the male turtle's arsenal of seduction techniques when looking for a mate. Some turtles may nudge or bite their intended partner, nuzzle their necks, or take a long sniff of the female's body. Turtles may display their colourful markings to attract attention, and can blow a stream of bubbles through the water towards the courted female.

Turtles have a reputation for being quiet creatures, but their mating is notoriously noisy. A red-footed tortoise (*Geochelone carbonaria*) makes clucking sounds while copulating, and Galápagos tortoises (*Chelonoidis nigra*) emit rumbling bellows. Sea turtles, once joined in mating, may copulate for more than 24 hours, with the female supporting the weight of the male while still taking in breaths of air. The male sea turtle must hold on to the female, as competitors may try to dislodge him and bite at his hindquarters.

Turtle mating in several species can be a violent affair, with the male and female turtles biting one another sufficiently hard to leave bleeding wounds. Male rivals may also bite one another or, on land, try to tip one another over. Male gopher tortoises competing for a female have been observed shoving one another and using their hind feet to kick sand into each other's faces, behaviour which may seem 'remarkably human'.[11] Even bystanders can be collateral damage in turtle mating. Well-meaning humans happening upon mating Galápagos tortoises have found themselves faced with a spitting and snapping animal that weighs over 250 kg (550 lb) and is protective of its privacy.[12]

Mating on dry land also has its hazards. Box turtles are known for their highly domed shells, into which they can defensively withdraw if under threat. During mating, however, the male needs to mount the female, which presents challenges from the creature's distinctive shape. The box turtle must lean over backwards while positioning himself for copulation, and must hook his toes into the edge of the female's lower shell to prevent himself from toppling over. The female can assist in this effort by holding him in place. Once anchored, the male tilts still further backwards until the shell touches the ground before inserting his penis into the female. At any time, a misjudged motion might tip the turtle onto his back, where he may die if unable to right himself.

The turtle's languid physical motions are reflected in its similarly unhurried progress through life. Turtles take a long time to mature – in some species, they can be over fifty years old before beginning to reproduce. Turtles are among a group of animals to experience very low rates of senescence as they age. 'Senescence' may be understood as symptoms of ageing, and often refers to functional decline in older age. A loss of reproductive capacity, senility or an increased mortality rate after reaching maturity may be considered as part of senescence. Turtles were once considered to show no senescence, but recent studies have shown that some species of turtle do exhibit signs of ageing – very slowly.

The long life span of some turtles and tortoises is a biological phenomenon with wide acceptance in the scientific community, yet ageing resistance in turtles is an area where 'surprisingly little' is known, even at the most basic level.[13] The accurate determining of a turtle's age remains a complicated and imprecise exercise. Gibbons notes particularly the difficulty of assessing the age of wild turtles caught in the field, and the historical lack of 'laboratory reptiles' that might illuminate the processes involved in turtle ageing.[14] The turtle's longevity is in this way an obstacle – if one were to attempt to track a turtle in the wild from hatching to natural death, one could be in for a very long wait.

Manouria emys, the Asian forest tortoise.

Despite these difficulties, it is clear that many turtles and tortoises have lived for remarkably long spans of time. In 2004 a Mediterranean spur-thighed tortoise named Timothy died at the age of 160 in her Devon castle home. The tortoise was named after a pet of the English naturalist Gilbert White, and was believed to be male until an unsuccessful mating attempt in 1926. Timmy was famously the last surviving witness to participate in the Crimean War – she was the mascot of HMS *Queen* during the first bombardment of Sevastopol in 1854. Other notably long-lived turtles included Adwaita, an Aldabra giant tortoise who died in Calcutta, India, in 2006 at an age of over 150. Adwaita's death made international news, as many believed Adwaita (whose name means 'the Only One') was the last survivor of four tortoises gifted to Lord Robert Clive of the British East India Company, which would have made him 255 years old at his death.

The oldest turtle in recorded history was Tu'i Malila, who died in 1966 at the age of 188. The radiated tortoise from Madagascar lived at the royal palace (and in its gardens) in Tonga, and he was traditionally believed to have been a gift from Captain James Cook to the royal family. In 2018 the world's oldest land animal currently living was believed to be a Seychelles giant tortoise (*Aldabrachelys gigantea hololissa*) named Jonathan, who was then 186 years old.

TURTLE BEHAVIOUR

Sea turtles can hold their breath while diving for hours at a time, and are the marathon swimmers of the sea. A 2014 study, using satellite tracking technology, revealed that green turtles can travel for over 4,000 km (2,500 mi.) without stopping for food – the longest distance ever recorded for marine animal migration.[15] Along with whale sharks, Arctic terns and grey whales, turtles are renowned for their remarkable migratory capacities.

The discovery of the green turtles' capacity for long-haul travel has 'rewritten the record books for long-distance marine animal migration'.[16] In 2008 a GPS tracker accompanied a leatherback turtle on a 649-day journey from Indonesia to Oregon. The turtle covered over 20,500 km (12,700 mi.) before the GPS was dislodged halfway back on the animal's return journey.

The turtle's capacity for long-haul travel means it may journey vast distances away from its place of hatching. Remarkably, most marine turtles will return even from their furthest travels to lay their eggs on the same beach on which they were hatched, showing what is known as 'philopatric' behaviour. 'Philopatry' is a zoological term that comes from Greek and translates as 'love of homeland'. The term refers to the habit of an animal to stay in or return to a particular geographic area.

Philopatry is an area of turtle behaviour which shows some differentiation between the sexes – while female turtles will return to the beach where they were hatched to reproduce, male turtles will not. Male sea turtles are generally less selective about the location of their reproduction than females, and may mate at multiple locations. This variety may reduce the potential for inbreeding among small populations of turtles inhabiting a limited area. The female's return home to the beach of her birth is thought to have developed to increase the chances of her offspring's survival. Beach selection can have crucial importance in providing hatchling turtles with an optimal chance of making their first trip from the beach to the water. A prime nesting site combines a happy confluence of environmental factors: it must not be too steep to exhaust the mother turtle on her way up the beach, and the sand must be suitable for her to dig a nest. A relatively low presence of predators, and other natural obstacles, can also assist the progress of the tiny turtle hatchlings.

A green sea turtle nesting on a beach on Heron Island, part of the Great Barrier Reef, at sunrise.

Leatherback sea turtle eggs in a nest.

A further consideration in nest site selection is the presence of parasites. A 2013 study showed female loggerhead turtles from different island regions had variances in their immune genes.[17] These differences gave them resistance to parasites from the individual turtle's home neighbourhood. The discovery could assist sea turtle conservation efforts, as allowing the female turtle to return to her 'home' beach could offer a survival advantage for her offspring.

Turtles can perceive the intensity of the earth's magnetic fields, and they use this sense to find their way. Hatchling turtles learn the location of their beach of origin through a process called geomagnetic imprinting, meaning they use magnetic fields as a kind of internal GPS.[18] This ability can be undermined by changes to a beach's magnetic signature, caused by alterations in its landscape. The addition of tidal breaks or housing along a shoreline augments the magnetic signature of a beach and potentially disorients animals using these fields for navigation.

The deepest divers among mammals are thought to be whales, namely the sperm whale and Cuvier's beaked whale. Turtles too are known for their capacity for deep diving. Among the various species of turtle, the leatherback holds the record for the deepest dives. The unique carapace (upper shell) of the leatherback turtle, made of thick, oily skin rather than shell, gives the animal increased flexibility under pressure at depth.

Dives by leatherback turtles have been recorded to exceed 1,000 m (3,300 ft) below the ocean surface. In 2006 a free-diving sea turtle off the South American coast was tracked diving to a depth of 1,186 m (3,891 ft).[19] The dive lasted almost an hour and a half, a new record for the longest recorded free-dive by a leatherback turtle. In 2008 a leatherback was recorded diving to an even greater depth, of 1,280 m (4,200 ft). As it seems unlikely that turtles reserve their deepest dives for those brief periods in which they are being scientifically tracked, it is probable that even greater depths have been reached by untracked leatherbacks in the wild. The exact reasons for deep diving in leatherback turtles are not clearly understood in the scientific community. Generally, leatherback dives last between ten and twenty minutes, and reach depths of no more than 250 m (820 ft).

To achieve their spectacular aquatic feats, turtles have numerous biological adaptations. Most vertebrate animals, such as humans, carry their shoulder and pelvic girdles outside of the main body cavity created by the ribcage. Turtles house their shoulder and pelvic girdles within their ribcage. This unique feature of turtle morphology is a significant departure from the standard skeletal plan among vertebrates, and is necessary for accommodating the turtle's shell.[20] While giving the turtle a good deal of protection, filling one's ribcage with connective girdles limits space for the lungs. For an animal with its shoulder girdle inside its ribcage, breathing, much less taking long, deep dives through water, is an impressive achievement.

Of course, the turtle is not the only armoured animal around. Other armoured creatures tend to have a tough protective layer on their backs, but a soft belly underneath. Armadillos (whose name comes from a Spanish word meaning 'little armoured one') have a soft underside which they can protect from predators by curling into a ball. Only turtles face the challenge of breathing 'while sealed, above and below, in a case of armour'.[21] Turtles cannot expand their ribs to breathe, as their ribs are fused to the shell.[22]

'Basking' is a behaviour in which an animal will position its body in a place where it will be exposed to warmth and sunlight. The causes of basking are diverse, but may include temperature regulation, maintenance and conditioning of the shell and skin, and parasite removal. Both turtles and tortoises bask, although the behaviour varies between species. A common activity for crocodiles and alligators, basking was once thought not to be part of sea turtle behaviour. In recent years, a greater understanding of sea turtles generally has led to the discovery that many species of sea turtle, such as the green turtle, the olive ridley and the leatherback turtle, bask, either on land or in the water, or both.[23]

Turtles often bask on rocks and logs, sandy beaches, grassy or muddy banks, or discarded lumber or concrete slabs. The utilization of less-common basking places is seemingly limited only by an individual turtle's creativity. Some rare basking spots recorded by scientists have included turtles on top of other turtles, on the backs of birds and on top of muskrat houses. In 1928 a turtle was observed basking on the head of a water buffalo that was almost entirely submerged.

In recent years, the behaviour of basking yellow-spotted river turtles (*Podocnemis unifilis*) in the Amazon has drawn global attention. The basking turtles draw crowds of butterflies, who flutter around the animals' faces, drinking their tears. The turtles' watering eyes are not thought to be due to the trying nature of life in the jungle, but a way for them to modulate the high sodium levels

Basking turtles.

in their systems, caused by their salt-rich diet. For the butterflies, the turtle tears provide an important source of sodium, which is lacking in their diet of flower nectar. Although greatly beneficial to the butterflies, the phenomenon of drinking turtle tears is largely limited to a small region in Ecuador.

Turtles and tortoises have excellent memories. The mechanisms through which sea turtles are able to navigate long distances back to the beach of their hatching are not as yet well understood, but it is thought that memory plays a role. Juvenile turtles have been shown to be able to remember the correct solution to puzzles for periods up to six weeks.

A recent study used red-footed tortoises to show that the long-term memory of the animals was much better than had previously been expected. In the study, tortoises trained to recognize distinctive visual clues related to food were able to remember and respond to the cues when tested eighteen months later.[24] The ability to remember a potential food source for long periods of time could be an important factor in a turtle's or tortoise's survival. The scientists were intrigued by the long life span of the tortoises, and wondered if they would need to retain information for longer periods of time than animals with briefer lives.

Turtles were long believed to be voiceless animals – in this aspect, they symbolized the cultural ideal of a silent and secluded wife in ancient Greece. Yet, contrary to Plutarch, turtles use a range of vocal communications. The vocalizations of land-dwelling turtles, such as chirruping Egyptian tortoises (*Testudo kleinmanni*), have been the subject of study for many years. Recently, marine turtles have added their voices to the discussion. A 2014 study found that Amazonian river turtles communicate through vocalizations, and talk to one another underwater. The parent turtles and hatchlings communicated with one another using sounds, with turtles using different sounds throughout the

Butterflies in Ecuador drinking turtle tears.

nesting season. The study marked the first recorded instance of parental care in turtles, proving that turtles are more complex socially than previously thought.[25]

In recent years, it has been accepted that all species of turtle can 'talk'. The Western Australian long-neck turtle (*Chelodina colliei*) has a vocal repertoire including complicated, percussive calls which are harmonically structured and frequency-modulated.[26] It is thought that through vocal communication, turtles can coordinate some of their behaviours, such as group basking. Studies of captive turtle populations in zoological parks have found turtles can participate in playful activities, further demonstrating that the understanding of turtle behaviour and cognition remains a work in progress.

The turtle, in its slow and unassuming manner, provides a living model of endurance and efficiency. While it may not set records for land speed, the turtle has proven its exceptionality by playing the long game – and in the process, setting remarkable benchmarks for distance swimming, deep diving and longevity. The turtle's ability to thrive in diverse environments likely provided an evolutionary advantage over other now-extinct animals from the

The underside of a turtle, from James de Carle Sowerby and Edward Lear, *Tortoises, Terrapins, and Turtles: Drawn from Life* (1872).

Cretaceous period. With their protective shells, opportunistic food gathering and 'striking anatomical and biological uniformity', turtles and tortoises have managed to persevere for many millions of years, from the Mesozoic to the modern day.[27]

The turtle's shell is its defining feature, and it has adapted to life in a suit of armour in unique and ingenious ways. The animal's ability to tolerate environmental extremes is reflected in the paradoxical quality of its own physiology. By turns hard and soft, bridging the divide between the earth and the ocean, the turtle's eclectic design gives it an essential, irreplaceable role in the earth's ecology.

2 Turtles in the Ancient World

There is more to life than increasing its speed.
Mahatma Gandhi

In the modern day, turtles are often considered to be gentle, passive creatures. These qualities, however, have not always dominated their image. In some of the world's earliest written records, turtles are presented as powerful and dangerous creatures, full of magical potency. While the Mesopotamians were developing the wheel and agriculture, and the Egyptians were building the pyramids, turtles of various shapes and sizes were swimming along the Nile and the Euphrates rivers, and basking by the water's edge. The influence of these half-shelled 'reptiles' can be seen in their appearance in early works of art and literature, and in their significant roles in the religious traditions of ancient cultures.

The liminal quality of the turtle, spanning the divide between water and land, has likely contributed to its prevalence as a supernatural symbol. The turtle's potency is often connected with protection and longevity, but at other times it is presented as a treacherous adversary for famous ancient heroes – and even, at times, for gods. For all their popularity as an artistic subject, turtles are not always presented in a flattering light. In the cultures of the ancient world, turtles play diverse roles – they are prominent symbolic referents or sources of food, and appear in medical texts and musical works. At other times, they are conspicuous by their absence.

Trionyx sp., fossil soft-shelled turtle in Eocene lacustrine marlstone, Wyoming.

As the home of one of the world's earliest civilizations, Mesopotamia is well suited as a starting point for a study on the ancient depictions of turtles. Along with sharing a reputation for antiquity, the name 'Mesopotamia' shows a similar geographical liminality to the turtles themselves. 'Mesopotamia' is a Greek word, meaning 'land between the rivers', and this name reflects the mixed environmental elements favoured by many turtles.

Recent archaeological research has shown the prominent role of the turtle in the Near East from Palaeolithic to post-Assyrian times. Evidence for turtles as a food source in the region is relatively scarce, with turtles seemingly playing an insignificant dietary role from the Neolithic onwards.[1] The evidence of turtle consumption better reflects magical uses, and they were also exploited for medical purposes.[2] One of the world's oldest known medical texts is a list of prescriptions from Mesopotamia that includes turtle shells. Along with the shells, milk, thyme and snakeskins are listed among a set of ingredients.[3]

Turtles played an important role in religion; their remains have been found at numerous burial sites throughout the Near East. The symbolic value of the turtle seems to have been fundamental to its usage, and they frequently appear as sacrificial offerings. Images of turtles, and their physical shells, had apotropaic uses. These uses included warding off evil and protecting dwellings and those who lived within them.[4] Votive items of gold and silver in the shape of turtles are listed in sacred dedications.

Turtles feature in omen texts. The literature contains portents describing places and situations in which it was inauspicious to see a turtle, and even signs connected to the turtle's direction of travel:

If a turtle crosses from a river to a marsh, water
will carry off that field in the commons.
If a turtle crosses from a marsh to a river, that
marsh will dry up; it will turn to arable land.[5]

Modern readers of the omen might imagine some anxious moments for Mesopotamian farmers waiting for crossing turtles to orient themselves.

Turtle omens in Mesopotamia can be related to city settings as well as rural ones. Indeed, there are many more omens relating to the city-slicker turtles than to their country kinfolk. One might imagine that turtles in ancient Mesopotamia would frequent urban settings less regularly than country ones, and if the omen texts are any indication, this is probably for the best. The appearance of turtles in city spaces seems to hold generally negative consequences in divination, as can be seen in the following omens.

If a turtle is seen in the city, that city will acquire
silence (of desolation). If a turtle is walking in the city
    square, that street
will become silent . . .
If a turtle is seen in a temple, that temple will be
abandoned . . . If a turtle enters a man's house, that house
    will be dispersed.[6]

Aside from omens, turtles also appear in narrative literature, such as the Sumerian myth of *Gilgamesh, Enkidu and the Netherworld*. They are listed among several other animals as part of a metaphor describing dangerous marine conditions faced by Enki, the god of wisdom and fresh water, following the creation of the world:

The keel of Enki's little boat was trembling as if it were being butted by turtles, the waves at the bow of the boat rose to devour the king like wolves and the waves at the stern of the boat were attacking Enki like a lion.[7]

While the turtles are the only animals in the metaphor to actually dwell in the water, the creatures seem to be collected together for their shared quality of ferocity. The capacity of turtles to butt into boats is likely to be based on historical observations of the animal's behaviour.

Enki and turtles are also paired in the myth of *Ninurta and the Turtle*. This Mesopotamian myth is another of the world's oldest works of literature, dating to early in the second millennium BCE. The story of Ninurta and the Turtle provides the first known literary example of the 'warrior turtle' motif, an image that has endured alongside the animal for millennia.

In the ancient story, the hero Ninurta is sent on a quest by Enki. Ninurta is to recover the Tablet of Destiny from a mythical

In a 9th-century BC bas-relief from Nineveh, Ninurta pursues the Anzud Bird in a scene from the Mesopotamian myth of Ninurta and the turtle.

46

Babylonian limestone *kudurru* depicting a turtle, which was a symbol of Enki.

beast, the Anzud Bird, who has stolen it. Ninurta is successful in retrieving the tablet. The deities tell Ninurta that he can name his reward, but Ninurta feels the best reward is simply to hang on to the tablet and gain control over the whole world. In response, Enki fashions an attack turtle from clay, and creates an ambush: the turtle sets upon Ninurta, and bites at his ankles. The turtle then digs a deep 'evil pit', into which the hero falls. The Tablet of Destiny is retrieved, the world is saved and the turtle continues its furious attack on Ninurta, tearing at him with its claws.

The animal's association with the god of wisdom extends beyond the world of literature. Turtles symbolized Ea (Enki in Sumerian myths) in the art of the Akkadian period, between 2350 and 2150 BCE.[8] Ea is at times symbolically represented by turtles on *kudurrus* – a type of carved stele or boundary stone used by the ancient Mesopotamians for numerous administrative, religious and political purposes.[9]

In the Mesopotamian myth of *The Turtle and the Heron*, the anthropomorphized turtle is criticized for its arrogance in challenging the heron. The turtle is described as a 'mud-brick', and an 'unwashed refuse basket'. Comparisons with other animals are used to describe parts of the turtle, which is said to have the eyes, mouth and tongue of a snake, and a 'puppy's bite'.

The descriptions of the turtle make an interesting contrast with the character of the heron. The heron builds her nest in the marshland and is described as the 'gift-giving' bird. The destructive turtle is described viciously attacking the creative heron:

> The turtle, the trapper of birds, the setter of nets, overthrew the heron's construction of reeds for her, turned her nest upside down, and tipped her children into the water. The turtle scratched the dark-eyed bird's forehead with its claws, so that her breast was covered in blood from it.[10]

The dispute between the heron and the turtle is only available in a fragmented state, creating some mystery around how the argument is resolved. Enki appears to decide the matter in favour of the bird. Part of Enki's remedy seems to involve building a secure area of the marsh for the heron to lay its eggs, suggesting an aetiological aspect to the story.

While turtles and herons were battling it out in the marshes of ancient Sumer, tortoises and cranes were more harmoniously paired in ancient myths from China. In Chinese myths, the strength of the turtle has a positive presentation. Indeed, the combination of a turtle (or tortoise) with a crane carried particularly good fortune, promoting longevity. Turtles are connected with wisdom in China, as in many cultures. The turtle's long life and the shape of its shell provided divine insights. The oval shape of its upper shell represented the heavens, and its lower shell the earth, allowing the animal to mediate between the human world and the divine.[11] This association inspired the widespread use of the turtle's shell in Chinese oracle bones.

Turtles feature in the writing of the legendary Taoist philosopher Chuang Tzu, who lived around the fourth century BCE. In the composition 'The Turtle', the seeking of high office and

Statue of the Chinese deity Zhenwu, with a turtle under his left foot, in Yangzhou.

49

honours is compared to a sacred turtle whose empty shell is the object of veneration. For the turtle, it is better to live, dragging its tail in the mud, than to give up its life in the search for approval and recognition.

Depictions of the Taoist deity Zhenwu, whose name means 'Perfected Warrior', involve the warrior with a tortoise and a snake. Zhenwu is found in Chinese culture from the third century BCE, when he is connected with the north and considered capable of powerful magic. The strength of the turtle was reflected in ancient Chinese sculpture, with stelae mounted on the backs of turtles becoming popular during the Han Dynasty. An early example of this type of monument was found in a tomb for a man named Fan Min in Lushan, dated to 205 BCE. The turtle monuments developed over time to be associated with the mythological figure Bixi, one of the nine sons of the Dragon King. Bixi,

A porcelain Taoist temple incense burner with the god Zhenwu, *c.* 1604.

depicted as a dragon with a turtle's shell, is known for his exceptional strength.

The Turtle is one of four sacred animals known for their intelligence, the other three being the Phoenix, the Qilin (a mythical hoofed creature) and the Dragon. These animals were believed by the Confucianists to bring luck. The Temple of Confucius in Qufu, Shandong Province, holds several turtle monuments that were installed during the Qing Dynasty. The turtles are over 4 m (13 ft) long, and the monuments weigh as much as 65 tonnes. In the Forbidden City, a bronze turtle representing one of the four sacred animals sits outside the Hall of Supreme Harmony.

The turtle and a Dragon King are also paired in Japanese mythology. In a well-known story, a fisherman named Urashima Tarō finds a turtle on a beach, being teased by children. Urashima purchases and frees the turtle. Later, a beautiful woman appears to the fisherman and leads him to the underwater Dragon Palace. The woman reveals that she is a princess, Otohime, and that she was the turtle he had rescued earlier.

TURTLES IN ANCIENT EGYPT

Returning to the Near East, we find turtles featured in Egyptian art and culture from early times. In ancient Egypt, the turtle's name had the meaning of 'the mysterious one'.[12] This name likely referred to river rather than land turtles. While generally beloved in the modern day, for ancient Egyptians the turtle was an enigmatic and fearsome creature. The ominous image of the turtle in Egypt is a rare example of the animal's perceived potency taking on a negative cast.

Egyptian river turtles have a reputation for secrecy. The turtles are active by night, and by using their noses as snorkels, they are capable of remaining submerged under water for extended periods

Palette depicting a pair of mud turtles from predynastic Egypt, c. 3650–3500 BCE.

of time. The combined qualities of inhabiting dark places and resting beneath the surface of the water place the turtle conceptually at odds with the Egyptian solar deity, Ra, who is associated with light. The turtle's sinister reputation in ancient Egypt meant its image was used for warding off other evils. Its image was also used symbolically to represent conflict between Egyptian deities. Ra had a daily battle with the Egyptian god of chaos, Apophis. Ra would sail through the sky and underworld on his boat, but his progress could be threatened by a thirsty turtle (sometimes a snake) who would drink the heavenly ocean, causing Ra's boat to run aground on Apophis' sandbank. The harpooning of an unfortunate turtle was also a feature of wall art in Egyptian tombs.

Images of turtles were featured on the wooden and bronze rods used by Egyptian magicians. Often referred to in the modern day as 'magic wands', these rods were held in the left hand by priests or magicians as they performed magic rites. Images of powerful animals, such as baboons, crocodiles and lions, and

Ancient Egyptian turtle as a votive object: front and back. Early Dynastic period, c. 3100–2649 BCE.

protective symbols such as the Eye of Horus decorated the sides of the magic wand, while the figure of the turtle was attached to the top end of the rod, to ward off harmful forces.[13]

BIBLICAL TURTLES

In light of their common religious use in the surrounding cultures of the ancient Near East, it is odd to learn that there are no overt references to turtles in the Bible. This omission may be suggestive of a taboo around the animals. It seems certain that the absence of biblical turtles did not result from their low numbers in ancient Canaan (a geographical space corresponding to present-day Israel and Palestine). At the site of Hilazon Tachtit, in Israel, an elderly woman was found buried with over fifty spur-thighed tortoises.[14] The burial is thought to date to around the eleventh millennium BCE, and the woman is believed to have been a shaman.[15]

Levantine turtles were useful for the living as well as the dead, with numerous bronze weights in the shape of turtles having been found in Israel, inscribed with ancient Hebrew. On the coastal plain of Israel, a turtle-shaped bronze with the inscription 'one-quarter shekel' has been discovered. This measurement is seen in the biblical book of 1 Samuel 9:8 – although of course, with no reference to a turtle.

Although not an explicit reference, it is thought that turtles may be included in the list of unclean foods from the books of Leviticus and Deuteronomy. The ambiguity of these passages has created modern controversy. In the last twenty years, conservationists have petitioned the Catholic Church to classify turtles as 'meat' rather than 'fish' to attempt to preserve their numbers. Reports in the *Chicago Tribune* and *Los Angeles Times* have noted the negative impact of consuming turtles during Lent as a meat substitute, a widespread tradition in parts of the southern United

States and Mexico.[16] Indeed, Pope John Paul II was asked to reclassify turtle as meat instead of fish to end their consumption during Lent by observant Catholics.

TURTLES IN THE CLASSICAL WORLD

Turtles appear on some of the earliest known minted silver coins from ancient Greece. The island of Aegina, in Greece's Saronic Gulf, south of Athens, had a turtle as the city's mascot featured on its coinage. By around 550 BCE, the distinctive Greek unit of currency known as the silver *stater* had begun to be produced on Aegina. These coins featured a square punch on the reverse and a turtle on the obverse. The modern Greek word for 'ingot' is *chelone* (turtle), possibly reflecting the ancient connection of the animals with currency.

Sea turtles made fitting ambassadors for Aegina's economy. Not only were they plentiful in the waters surrounding the island, but Aegina itself was a centre for maritime trade. With the decline of Aegina as a maritime power towards the mid-fifth century BCE, and the rise of Athens, the turtles on the coins from Aegina were replaced with land tortoises. The flippers of the marine turtle were substituted for the feet of the tortoise, most likely the common Greek tortoise (*Testudo graeca*).[17]

Silver 'turtle' coin from Aegina, c. 510–500 BCE.

Turtles in ancient Greece were associated with the goddess of love, Aphrodite. Statues of Aphrodite Urania are described by the Greek geographer Pausanias as presenting the deity with one foot resting on a turtle.[18] This classical image was referenced in the writings of the famous naturalist John James Audubon (1785–1851). Encountering a loggerhead turtle, he was taken with its incredible size, observing how its shell would make a kind of 'curious carriage' or 'a car on which Venus herself might sail over the Caribbean sea'.[19]

Another silver 'turtle' coin from Aegina, from the same period.

Silver 'turtle' coin from Aegina.

According to Plutarch, the combination of turtles and Aphrodite relates to the traditional marital role of women in ancient Greek culture. This role involved staying in the home (presumably considered an easy feat for the shelled chelid) and staying quiet.[20] The associations between turtles, women, silence and domesticity are prominently featured in classical myths involving the wedding of the Greek gods Hera and Zeus. In Aesop's fables, all the animals receive an invitation to the wedding of the two deities, and the tortoise alone declines. The animal cites its love of its dear, familiar home as the reason for its non-attendance. Zeus responds by ordering the creature to carry her home with her wherever she goes.

The fearsome qualities of the turtle, widely recognized in ancient Near Eastern myth, are also found in myths from the classical world. The Greek hero Theseus encounters a dangerous turtle on his legendary travels. Theseus is likely best known as the hero who entered King Minos' labyrinth and slew the monstrous Minotaur. Theseus' myths tend to involve either the hero abducting women, fighting local tyrants or battling monsters, and occasionally, all three at once.

The presence of a turtle monster in Theseus' fight with Sciron is an interesting departure from the largely human-centred trials of the Athenian hero.[21] Sciron is portrayed as a tyrannical bandit who lives on a clifftop. When travellers pass his way, he makes them kneel before him and wash his feet. Once they are crouched in a vulnerable posture, Sciron kicks the travellers off the cliff and into the sea, where they are attacked and eaten by a monstrous turtle. In the myth, Theseus defeats Sciron and then casts him into the same sea that is patrolled by the giant turtle, meaning that he is likely consumed by the creature in the end. Several representations of the fight between Theseus and Sciron have been preserved in ancient Greek art. Many portray the unhappy bandit falling

Third-century
statue of Aphrodite
and a turtle.

Athenian bowl
decorated with
the turtle myth
of Sciron and
Theseus.

from the cliffs, and the hungry turtle lurking below. Pausanius recounts the myth in his *Description of Greece*, with added zoological details: 'Sea tortoises are like land tortoises except in size and for their feet, which are like those of seals.'[22]

The messenger deity, Hermes, is said to have created a musical instrument from a turtle. The precocious son of Zeus and Maia, Hermes' first act on the day of his birth is to kill a turtle and build a lyre from its shell. The *chelys*, a Greek stringed instrument, received its name from the mythical connection to turtles, and the lyre itself was often formed with a shell soundbox. The mythical connection between turtles and lyres generally ended poorly for the classical animal, but an exception can be found in a passage from Pausanias. On Mount Parthenion in Arcadia, Pausanias observes that native tortoises are well suited for the creation of lyres. The turtles of the region, however, were sacred to the wilderness deity Pan, so the local people would not allow them to be captured.

The usefulness of turtle shells for making lyres was also one of the animal's most important aspects in Roman culture, and it was further valued for its ornamental properties. In the works of Ovid, Virgil and Lucan, the decorative display of tortoiseshell inlays is linked to displays of wealth.[23] In the *Augustan History*, a late Roman collection of biographies of uncertain authorship, babies in the imperial family are said to have bathed in tortoiseshell tubs.[24]

The connection between turtles and musical instruments stretches back beyond the world of ancient Greek myth. Since prehistoric times, Native Americans have used turtle rattles for ceremonial functions. Rattles made from turtle shell may also have had apotropaic functions, in protecting the community from evil.[25] Musical instruments made from turtle shells were used by the Tukano people of the northwestern Amazon, the use of the instrument thought to have related to myths of sexuality and fertility.[26] Turtle shells were also prominently used in Aztec, Mixtec and Mayan societies in the making of the *ayotl* drum. The word *ayotl* means 'turtle' in Nahautl, and these percussion instruments were played by striking the shell with either a mallet or deer antler,

Limestone statue of a temple boy holding a tortoise. Cyprus, 5th century BCE.

causing sound to resonate through the carapace.[27] Modern Tzotzil Maya use maize cobs to strike turtle drums.[28]

'Turtle power' may appear to be a modern phenomenon, relating more to cartoon characters than to slow-moving chelids. Yet turtles have been recognized as powerful creatures from prehistoric times. In ancient religions, the symbol of the turtle could forewarn of impending danger, and in cult practices the animal was used to ward off evil. The might of the turtle in antiquity did not relate only to its ability to succeed in battle. The turtle frequently represented knowledge and longevity. In many cultures, the animal was conceptually tied to wisdom traditions and wisdom deities, divination, oracles and fate. The creature's reptilian power was put to further use in the fields of medicine and magic. The animals' association with strength and sagacity has continued into their modern-day image.

Finally, the frequent association of turtles with music and dancing through many millennia contrasts with the creature's quiet image in some myths. The frequent use of turtle instruments in religious practices shows the diversity and surprisingly mellifluous qualities of the animal's power.

Turtle-shell Aztec drum (top right) from the mid-16th century *Codex Magliabecchi*.

3 Turtles, Culture and Community

The tortoise does not have milk to give, but it knows how to care for its child.
Ashanti proverb

The modern image of the turtle, symbolizing ecological balance, draws deeply on its association as a powerful warrior in the ancient world, and its mythical connection with protecting the earth and conserving its natural order. In many cultures, turtles are involved in the creation and order of the cosmos: in the Chinese myth of the goddess Nu Gua, the deity created humanity and used the legs of a sea turtle to repair the pillars of heaven.[1] While the animal's antiquity and anatomical sturdiness uniquely qualify it as a world-bearer, its perceived wisdom and compassion also inform its creative role. These qualities see the turtle featuring in myths involving the importance of family and community – ancient, wise and placid, the turtle at times assumes the role of a kindly animal elder.

The variety of roles played by turtles in world religions and folklore reflects their natural complexity. Myths and legends involving turtles show sophisticated interplay with the biological reality of the animal, such as in its natural role bringing nutrients and minerals from the sea to the land. The turtle's wisdom is generally shaped positively, lending the creature patience and understanding, but at times may include darker traits of trickery and deception. From the warrior turtle archetype, to the close connection with world-building, the power of the turtle is by turns destructive and creative. Strong, steady and slow-moving, the

The image of a turtle decorates a Mola blouse. Panama, 20th century.

turtle's varied roles in global cultures illustrate its subtle natural qualities and unique ties to its natural environment.

Often seen as a warrior associated with destructive power, the turtle is also recognized in many myths for its creative potential. This power is clearly seen in the frequent mytheme of the World Turtle. This mythical motif, involving a turtle carrying the world upon its back, is found across a variety of cultures and historical settings. For many turtles, the ability to inhabit terrestrial and aquatic environments is a biological reality, and the recognition of this quality of the animal may contribute to the popularity of the image.

The carrying of the world by the turtle is an act of selflessness and altruism – the world is heavy, and carrying it is no easy task. The arduous nature of the job is shown in numerous variations of the myth involving the turtle giving a shrug when tired (leading to earthquakes). The turtle stretching under its burden for a temporary reprieve is a feature of the Mohawk myth involving the World Turtle.

Numerous myths, including those from many Native American cultures, emphasize the kindness of the turtle, and its concern for other creatures, in the origins of its cosmic role. This makes an interesting contrast with other well-known earth-carriers, such as Atlas. In Greek myth, the Titan Atlas is given the task of holding up the earth as a divine punishment. Unlike Atlas, the World Turtle is generally presented volunteering for the role of earth-holder, if the origins of its involvement are included as part of the myth. The burdensome nature of carrying the world leads Atlas to attempt to trick the Greek hero Herakles (Roman Hercules) to trade places with him. Despite the odd tired shrug, the World

Turtle generally accepts the long-term commitment of its laborious role.

The World Turtle is also entrusted with carrying the earth due to the animal's reputation for steadiness. The turtle's wide-ranging reputation for antiquity and longevity aligns well with its timeless role.

As well as being a world-bearer, the sturdiness and endurance of the turtle has seen it symbolize the surface of the earth.[2] A giant turtle (alternatively at times a caiman) swimming in a primordial sea was thought to represent cosmic space in Mayan myths. The high cosmic status of the turtle saw it used in the visual representation of numerous deities. Scenes representing the resurrection of the Mayan maize deity feature turtle symbolism, including images of turtle shells inhabited by *Bacabs* (also called *Pauahtuns*). *Bacabs* are four aged pre-Hispanic deities associated with the interior of the earth and its waters. They are sometimes called the 'Skybearers'. The scene of the grain deity's resurrection

The geographic turtle, from *Birds and All Nature* magazine (1899).

is considered the most important context of turtle shells in Mayan art.[3] A common feature of the scene is the eruption of the Maize God from the cracked surface of the earth, which is represented by a split turtle shell carrying a water lily motif.[4]

Turtles appear in various Mayan codices, as well as murals, vases, other works of art and even constellations. In the Mayan cosmic worldview, the turtle is represented by parts of the constellation known as Orion in Western astrology, specifically, Orion's belt. The turtle in Mayan cosmology might be associated with the Western zodiac sign of Gemini, due to the Earth's precession over time (the 'wobble' of the earth on its axis).[5] This is a continual motion caused by the gravitational attraction of the Moon, and the effect is a kind of slippage of the zodiac signs from their initially recognized locations. An early colonial dictionary of Mayan words connects three stars from Gemini with the Mayan turtle constellation.

The Mayan zodiac appears in the Paris Codex. This book is one of three surviving pre-Columbian Mayan records, dating from around 900–1500 CE. The Mayan zodiac had thirteen houses, and the first three of these houses in the Paris Codex are the Scorpion, Turtle and Rattlesnake.[6] Turtles can be found in various parts of the famous Madrid Codex, another of the three surviving pre-Columbian Mayan records. The stellar turtle is seen in numerous Mayan artworks, including the famous Bonampak murals. In a scene from the Bonampak murals, a turtle is shown with three stars shining on its back, highlighting its celestial qualities.

Further north, the World Turtle plays a central role in indigenous culture and thought. North America is known among indigenous communities as 'Turtle Island'. This name stems from a creation myth, which survives in numerous versions. In the Haudenosaunee myth, Sky Woman falls through a hole in the sky.

She is lifted on the wings of geese to save her from falling into the water below. Small animals dive deep into the water until one of them succeeds in returning to the surface with mud. The mud is placed on the back of a turtle, to provide a strong surface for Sky Woman, and it becomes Turtle Island (now known as North America).[7]

The story of the turtle providing the foundations for life on land is also told in a myth from the Hitchiti tribe of the Apalachicola people, a Native American community based around modern-day Florida. In this origin myth, a story is told of a world filled with water, without any land. The water covers the animals seeking shelter in the shallows, and Turtle is moved to help them. Turtle's efforts to help the other animals involve several stages, resulting in the development of the land, the sun and the art of dancing.

In the first part of Turtle's plan, she raises her head from the waters and calls the other animals near so that they might hear her instructions. Then she shows the other animals how to swim. When the other animals tire, she allows them to rest on her back. Next, she swims deep into the water to retrieve earth for land:

> While all the others were swimming, Turtle dived beneath the waters and found land. She scooped it up and brought it to the surface. Soon every creature living had a little bit of land. Everyone began to pile their land up together. Winds helped drive the water back to the edge. Creator, One Above, smiled at things working together – that smile was the Sun. All things still lived together in the early days; everything spoke the same sound and understood each other. Together they decided to hold a dance to honor Turtle.
>
> It was the very first dance.[8]

Although turtles are viewed in myth as having helped humans since the time of the origins of the world, it is thought that the animals have yet to finish their job in assisting their human friends. Turtles are said to continue to teach and help humans about the value of patience, and the importance of avoiding 'hurry-waste'.[9] The turtle demands respectful treatment from humans, who are in the creature's debt. This respectful attitude can be shown through actions such as helping turtles to cross the road.

Turtles in Native American myth are connected intimately with time – they are present at the beginning of creation and teach the value of moving slowly, and their lives span great expanses of time. The turtle is also connected to time by its shell. Turtles' shells were used as the first calendars by North American Indians. The thirteen scutes on the back of an eastern box turtle were associated with the thirteen moons (months) that appeared before the return of the same season. The turtle carried the thirteen moons on its oval back in a sacred hoop, or medicine wheel. This wheel represented the circle of life, the path of the earth around the sun, and could guide humans along their path through life.[10]

The World Turtle, seen in legends from North America, is also found in Hindu religion. In Hinduism, the world is carried on the backs of four elephants, who are supported on the back of a giant turtle. The Hindu deity Vishnu also takes the form of a tortoise in the second of his ten avatars. Turtles in Hindu mythology could also represent creative power.

The slow movements of the turtle, and its appearance in ancient Indian wisdom traditions, perhaps make its appearance in the practice of yoga unsurprising. Kashyapa, whose name means 'Turtle', was an important Vedic sage, one of the seven *rishi*s thought to have composed the ancient verses of the Rigveda

Tibetan blood-letting calendar, depicting a turtle and other animals. The calendar was also used to warn of times when it was necessary to guard against demons. The turtle is flanked by protector deities.

text. In yoga, the *Kashyapa*, or Turtle, *mudra* (hand gesture) involves placing the thumb between the middle and ring fingers of the hands, and making a fist. This *mudra* is thought to balance masculine and feminine energies, and to help clear negative energies or spirits. The yogic pose *Kurmasana* means 'turtle pose', and is one of the Ashtanga primary series. The pose promotes inward contemplation, and peace of mind. It is thought to provide the

Statue depicting the deity Vishnu's turtle avatar in Tirumala, India.

practitioner with relief from outward agitation – like a turtle finding shelter by retreating into its shell. The pose requires a great deal of flexibility in the hips, lower back, and hamstrings, especially for the more advanced version of the pose, *Supta Kurma-sana* (Sleeping Turtle Pose), which involves moving the feet behind the head.

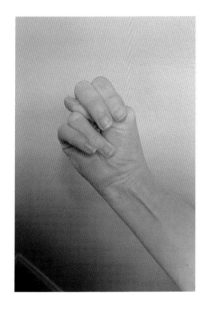 

POLYNESIAN TURTLES

The islands of Polynesia have a long history of cultural connections between humans and turtles. For many Polynesian coastal communities, the turtle is a 'flagship species' of tremendous cultural and spiritual importance.[11] The World Turtle is also found in myths from Polynesia, where in some stories, humans are said to be born from eggs laid by the legendary creature.[12]

Transformation is at the heart of the famous Samoan legend of the turtle and the shark (known as *O Le Tala I Le Laumei Ma Le Malie* in Samoan). In this story, two humans face great difficulty, and then throw themselves from a high cliff. Instead of dying upon hitting the water, the two are changed into animals, meaning their deep love lives on forever. The relationship between the human characters, the cause for their dive from the cliff and even

The turtle hand *mudra*, considered to defend against harmful energy and provide balance.

Australian yoga teacher Lisa Theodore demonstrates the advanced yoga pose *Kurmasana*. The pose promotes inward contemplation and peaceful thoughts.

the animals involved show some variation. In one version, the two are family members, a grandmother and her granddaughter, shunned by their tribe during a time of famine. To avoid starvation, the two jump from the cliffs and are changed into a turtle and a shark. This version, with some changes, was recorded by missionary George Turner in 1884, although he believed the story related to two turtles. The anthropologist Margaret Mead also referred to this version of the legend.[13]

The Samoan narrative has ties to the geographical landscape of the islands. There is a cove in American Samoa, called Turtle and Shark (*Laumei ma Malie*). This area is recognized for its heritage value in preserving the cultural traditions of the American Samoan community.

The Hawaiian Islands hold numerous turtle myths and legends. The Hawaiian deity 'Ai'ai is credited with creating a *honu* ('turtle'), in an aetiological story explaining the origins of turtles. 'Ai'ai is the son of the Hawaiian fishing deity Ku'ula-kai and his wife Hina-puku-i'a, and he is known to have an important role in establishing fishing grounds and practices. While on the island of Lāna'i, 'Ai'ai carves a *honu* from a rock, and calls upon his father and mother for help in bringing it to life. The story explains how turtles came to Hawaii, and why they return to land to nest – that is where the first turtle was 'born' from rock. The place where the *honu* came to life is called Polihua.

The origins of turtles in Hawaii are the focus of another narrative. In the legend of Kana and Niheu, a giant turtle takes the form of the hill known as Ha'upu. The turtle's name is Kahonunuimaeleka (or Maeaea). Kahonunuimaeleka holds the goddess Hina captive, but her son Kana fights to free her. This *mo'olelo* (story/legend) tells how turtles came to be in Hawaii – Kana chops the hill into little bits to rescue his mother, and each of the pieces becomes a turtle.

Some '*ohanas* ('families') in Hawaii consider the *honu* to be an '*aumākua* or ancestral guardian. Families who acknowledge this lineage and tradition would not engage in any activity which might harm a turtle. The caring treatment between families and their guardians flows in both directions. It is thought that if a family member connected with a *honu* were to be in distress in the ocean, their animal guardian would surface and provide them with help.[14]

Turtles also play a significant role in Melanesian culture. The graceful movements of the turtle, swimming under water, are referenced in Fijian mythology, where a goddess who wishes to fly transforms into a giant turtle. Turtle myths are celebrated through the practice of 'turtle calling' by the people of the Namuana Village on Kadavu Island. The villagers perform a sacred ceremony wearing leis and leaf skirts, and they climb onto the hills and sing for the goddess and her daughter to visit them. In the associated myth, the goddess and her daughter become separated, and the

Basking green turtle on Punaluu Beach on Hawaii's Big Island.

Green Island Melanesian turtle sculpture.

daughter transforms into a turtle. The mother goddess mourns for her daughter on the beach, before she is also transformed, leading to the pair's reunion. Through 'turtle calling', the appearances of the goddesses, in turtle form, are a symbol of protection for the community.

OTHER TURTLE LORE

Japan has a distinctive cultural relationship with turtles, and one which has proved greatly influential at an international level. Turtles feature in the artistic works of Katsushika Hokusai (1760–1849), from the Edo period.

The *minogame* is a mythical turtle with a distinctively long, brushy tail that symbolizes the seaweed that has accumulated on the turtle's back during its long life. The *minogame* is sometimes called the 'thousand years' turtle due to its exceptionally long life

74

span. At times, the *minogame* is pictured with deities, or other animals. In Japanese art from many periods, turtles and cranes are paired as a sign of happiness and longevity.

Tortoises often featured in netsuke, distinctive miniature sculptures created in Japan in the seventeenth century. Netsuke were created to solve a practical problem – the absence of pockets in kimonos. They were formed like small boxes, often carved from ivory, and were hung from cords to hold personal items, but became known for their artistic merit. Netsuke often depict mythical figures, such as the Seven Lucky Gods, believed to grant luck and bring good fortune. One of the seven, Fukurokuju, is a deity

Katsushika Hokusai (1760–1849), depiction of a turtle.

Kappa water-imp riding a turtle, by Naitō Toyomasa (Japan, 1773–1856).

connected with wisdom. Fukurokuju is considered the patron of chess players, and is frequently depicted accompanied by a turtle.

Turtles appear in many forms in Japanese culture, but one of the best-known mythical turtle-like creatures is the *kappa*. Present in traditional Japanese folklore, *kappa* are green-skinned, turtle-backed river imps that are depicted behaving in mischievous or unpredictable ways. While part of Japanese culture for hundreds of years, in the modern day the creature is being represented in new and creative ways. A 2016 tourism campaign for the city of Nobeoka used a *kappa* and a *ningyo* (a creature that is part human and part fish, and often referred to as a Japanese mermaid) to attract people to the city.[15]

The connection between turtles and mermaids extends beyond the world of advertising. The Mesoamerican storm deity, Tezcatlipoca, is assisted by his three helpers in an aetiological myth: a turtle, a whale and a mermaid.[16] Interestingly, the myth involves the creation of music in the world, and the turtle features alongside two other marine creatures known for their abilities to create beautiful songs.

A turtle is the trusted companion of a mermaid in a story from South Korean folklore. In the story, Princess Hwang-Ok ('Topaz') marries a prince and becomes human. She is filled with home-sickness until advised by her turtle companion to look up at the moon through an enchanted piece of topaz.[17] This action causes her to turn back into a mermaid and regain her well-being.

Australia's natural ecological richness is reflected in its wealth of turtles: of seven species of marine turtles in the world, six occur in Australian waters. In ancient Aboriginal narratives, the turtle's distinctive physiology has played a role in its characterization in mythology. The popular myth of Wayamba the Turtle gives an aetiological account of how the turtle came to live in the water.

Rock painting of a turtle, Kakadu National Park, Australia.

Wayamba is a turtle who kidnaps the wife and children of a lizard. The turtle's actions anger his tribe, who threaten him with spears. The turtle slings on two of the biggest shields he can find, one at the front, and one at the back. He dives into the water for further protection, drawing his head and limbs in behind the safety of the two shields. In this way, the turtle comes to be at home in the waters of Australia.

The word *wayamba*, an indigenous name for 'turtle', has been used by Australia's Defence Science and Technology Organization (DSTO) for a remote-controlled, underwater military vehicle. The craft was designed for espionage work, and also potentially to deliver supplies to sunken submarines.[18]

THE TRUTH ABOUT TURTLES

The remarkable ability of the turtle to gracefully inhabit the earth's terrestrial and aquatic zones has captured the human imagination for millennia. A deep awareness of the biological reality of the turtle is reflected in many of its mythical roles. The animal is presented bringing forth the land from the water, and in doing so, promoting and protecting life on earth, in all of its diversity. This mythic quality aligns with the natural role of turtles in the environment. Turtles have often been overlooked for their importance in seed dispersal, and assisting in the healthy germination of plants. By transporting and depositing seeds (via their digestive systems), turtles influence the types and numbers of plants in their ecosystems and play a vital role in the maintenance of terrestrial ecosystems.

As well as helping to fuel the growth of plants, turtles also bridge the divide between land and aquatic environments through nesting on beaches. This role, reflected in the narratives of many ancient myths, provides a significant movement of energy, minerals and nutrients between marine and terrestrial environments.[19] Turtles further assist in the growth of terrestrial plants, and the redistribution of energy, through burrowing. In the process of burrowing, turtles contribute to 'bioturbation', meaning that they contribute to the formation, function and maintenance of soil.[20]

The turtle, it would seem, really does carry a small world on its shell. Recent scientific research has shown that the mythological trope of the Creator Turtle, carrying the world on the back of its shell, is a figure with roots in biological reality. Studies involving sea turtles have found that the animals carry a variety of small creatures called 'epibionts' on their backs. The word 'epibiont' comes from ancient Greek, and means 'living on top of'. The descriptive term 'epibiont' is used to describe a host of tiny organisms that make their homes on the surface of other organisms. All seven species of sea turtle carry communities of epibiota.[21] The relationships between the turtle mariners and their tiny crew of shell-dwellers are a complex and developing field of research. Some of the small organisms may provide their turtle host with benefits, such as the removal of old skin, or the presence of barnacles may provide the turtle with camouflage. Others may have a negative impact: for example, barnacles may grow over the turtle's eyes and obscure its vision, or a large group of barnacles might create 'drag' in the water, slowing the turtle down (more so).

Each of the tiny worlds transported on top of turtles is distinctive. A 2017 study of olive ridley, leatherback and green sea turtles in Costa Rica found that each species held unique epibiont communities.[22] The presence of a distinctive epibiont can be considered a type of biological 'souvenir', directing researchers to areas through which the host turtle has travelled. This information in turn has value for guiding efforts towards the management and conservation of turtles and their habitats.[23] Of course, this research benefits more than just the turtle – it can also assist in the survival of whole tiny worlds that ride on the animal's back.

Turtles have not commonly been known for their sociability in modern behavioural science, yet many cultural representations of turtles emphasize the importance of strong social bonds. The growing awareness of turtle communications in the scientific world aligns well with the animal's appearance in myth and legend. Turtle myths also tend to connect the creatures to music and dancing – allowing for a more nuanced perspective on an animal often viewed as silent and still. The consideration of the turtle's more subtle qualities, seen in myths and legends, reflects a deep engagement with this ancient creature, and shows how much remains to be discovered about the turtle and its world.

4 Turtles, Trade and Technology

All the thoughts of a turtle are turtle.
Ralph Waldo Emerson

Turtles are some of the most widely travelled animals on earth – rivalling even some species of whale. With their broad territorial range, turtles have played a significant role assisting in the expansion of human exploration and the development of global trade. Turtle shells have been traded for millennia, and the animals have provided sea explorers with meat, eggs and leather. The overexploitation of turtles in the seventeenth century led to a sharp decline in their numbers, and consequently these dwindling turtle populations played an important role in the genesis of the environmental conservation movement.

TURTLES AND MODERN MEDICINE

The relationship between humans and turtles is often one-sided in terms of benefits, yet recent times have shown the potential for a more balanced relationship. The pairing of humans and turtles in the field of medical research and technology promises to greatly benefit both species. The connection between turtles and human healing is one that extends back into antiquity and continues in the field of modern medicine.

Recent research has shown that turtles, like humans, can experience unfortunate side effects from treatment with antibiotic medications. Turtles being treated for bacterial infections by

A hawksbill sea turtle swimming in the ocean.

Queensland-based researchers developed stomach upsets and were unable to digest seagrass. The turtles also showed a high prevalence of multidrug-resistant bacteria.[1] The presence of antibiotic resistance in the green turtles studied has implications that spread beyond the unwell animals, as it is indicative of the swift evolution of multidrug-resistant genes in the environment.

To address these problems, the researchers worked to treat the turtles' bacterial infections with phage therapy. Although not widely used in the present day, phage therapy is over a century old, with its usage pre-dating that of penicillin. The therapy was discovered between 1915 and 1917, and was used to treat bacterial infections in the 1920s and 1930s. Phage therapy involves the targeted use of bacterial viruses to infect and destroy bacterial cells – it is estimated that there are over 10 million trillion trillion phages in the world. The turtles' phage therapy was highly successful in addressing the animals' antibiotic resistance, and facilitating their recovery to good health. Phage therapy is hoped to become a new (old) weapon in the fight against human antibiotic resistance.

In 2018 a study demonstrated that a particular form of cancer in turtles could possibly be treated with medicines designed for humans.[2] The type of tumour is caused by the herpes-like virus *fibropapillomatosis*, but is also connected to environmental degradation, such as increasingly polluted water and exposure to more ultraviolet light.[3] The tumours present a global risk to already threatened species of wild turtle, having been first observed by marine biologists in the Florida Keys in the 1930s. Recent work profiling the turtle tumours has found shared genetic vulnerabilities with human cancers, making treatment with human anti-cancer therapeutics amenable. Treating sea turtles with human anti-cancer drugs has led to dramatic improvements in reducing the recurrence of the tumours after removal.[4]

Turtle swimming off the Great Barrier Reef.

Like humans, turtles have been fighting cancer for a very long time. In 2019 researchers working with the fossil of an extinct turtle ancestor discovered evidence of bone cancer in the animal's leg. The 240-million-year-old fossil dates to the Triassic period, and is the oldest known example of this type of cancer in an amniote (a group including reptiles, birds and mammals).[5] The prehistoric cancer was found to bear very strong similarities to a type of bone cancer that appears in modern humans. The discovery illustrates the interconnectedness of all inhabitants of earth's biosphere, as noted by one of the authors of the study:

> We are one community which responds to the environment and whatever factors that cause cancer in the same way . . . We're all part of the same Earth and we are all inflicted with the same phenomena.[6]

The remarkable ability of turtles to survive without oxygen for long periods of time has captured the attention of medical researchers. Recent research suggests that understanding the turtle's capacity for tolerating extreme environmental conditions

Tammy, a 114-kg (252 lb) loggerhead turtle, receives medical aid from scientists.

A rescued teenage sea turtle.

without oxygen has the potential to help humans to better survive heart attacks. During a heart attack, the lack of oxygen being transported through the human body can cause cells to die, damaging the heart. Scientists have shown that turtles in an environment without oxygen inhibit the functions of the mitochondria in their cells, protecting them from sustaining damage. This new finding may help to protect human hearts, and improve their capacity to heal.

Another recent discovery has shed new light on the turtle itself. In 2015 a species of turtle in the South Pacific was found to be the first biofluorescent 'reptile' ever found in the wild. The discovery was made by marine biologist David Gruber, while filming biofluorescent sharks and corals in the Solomon Islands. While watching out for the crocodiles native to the area during a dive, Gruber encountered a glowing hawksbill sea turtle (*Eretmochelys imbricata*). The turtle glowed red and green, and it has been suggested the behaviour may provide the animal with camouflage.[7]

In recent years, bionic turtles with prosthetic flippers have been proving successful candidates for rehabilitation after injury. After losing limbs from boat-strike or attacks from predators, damaged turtles have been fitted with replacement flippers, learned to swim again and been released into the ocean. Working with turtles helps scientists to develop further knowledge and precision which can then be transferred to the growing field of human prosthetics.

TURTLES AND TRADE

Turtles are the ocean's ancient mariners – exploring great depths, fishing for food and tending to fields of seagrass like flippered gardeners of the sea. These ancient creatures have contributed immensely to human sea exploration, leaving their mark on human history. Turtle meat was a nutritious source of protein for explorers, and the animals were easily kept alive on board ships for long periods at sea. In the early days of sea exploration to the New World, turtles were abundant, and numerous ships' logs note the frequent stopping on islands mid-voyage in order to 'take on turtles'.

In 1502 the Italian explorer Christopher Columbus set out on his fourth and final voyage to the New World, and in 1503 he arrived at the Cayman Islands. Columbus was so impressed with the large number of turtles in the area that he named the islands 'Las Tortugas' (the turtles). Ferdinand Columbus, the explorer's son, wrote in his diary that the sea and the islands were so full of turtles that they looked like small rocks. At an earlier point in his seafaring career, Christopher Columbus encountered a leper colony in the Cape Verde islands where the patients were thought to receive medicinal benefits from eating turtle meat and bathing in their blood. The practice is described in the *History of the Indies*, a volume created by the colonist and social reformer Bartolomé de las Casas in 1527, who observed that turtles around the islands were 'as big as shields'.

Despite explorers' observations of vast numbers of turtles, the exploitation of the animals caused a free fall in their populations. In 1610 the large numbers of turtles on Bermuda were noted by William Strachey in his account of the shipwreck of the *Sea Venture*. In his report of the wreck of the colonial ship, Strachey noted how the turtles provided a vital food source for the stranded colonists. Just over a decade later, in 1620, turtle numbers in Bermuda had fallen so rapidly that an Act was passed on the island to limit their slaughter. This Bermudian Act is the world's earliest marine turtle conservation legislation, and a landmark event in the genesis of the conservation movement. The rapid decline of the green turtles of Bermuda was recorded by famous zoologist and 'turtle man' Archie Carr, in his *Handbook for Turtles*.[8] Carr observed waning turtle numbers around the Cayman Islands, and in the waters around Florida.

Bermuda's efforts to protect its turtle population were followed in 1711 by a law passed in Jamaica protecting turtle eggs.[9] In 1907 two more laws were passed protecting sea turtles as well as their eggs. Further legislation aimed at protecting turtles and other animals was provided by Jamaica's Wildlife Protection Act of 1945.

The navigator and explorer William Dampier observed that turtles were exploited by pirates as well as explorers. Many Dutch and English pirate ships, he noted, would carry a Miskito person (a member of a Central American indigenous community) to harpoon turtles, as the Miskito were renowned for their aim. Hunting turtles, or 'turtling', was a common practice during the golden age of piracy, as it had been earlier among Elizabethan buccaneers, such as Sir Henry Morgan. The pirate Anne Bonny was frustrated in her pursuit of revenge due to a turtling expedition. Richard

A hawksbill sea turtle, from Mark Catesby's *Natural History of Carolina* (1743).

Turnley, who Bonny felt had betrayed her, was hunting for turtles when Bonny and Jack Rackham ('Calico Jack') came looking. Turnley's crew, waiting on the turtle sloop, escaped with a warning. On a separate occasion in 1719, Rackham deposed the English pirate Charles Vane as captain of his ship and set him adrift on a rowboat. Vane managed to make his way to a deserted island, where he survived through the generosity of local turtle hunters.

It was not only naval explorers and pirates who relied on turtles to survive inhospitable environments. In the 1850s, San Francisco was hit with a population explosion brought about by the gold rush. Settlers who arrived in the pursuit of gold swiftly exhausted the area's other natural resources – such as the native wildlife. The population of native elk in California was almost driven to extinction by hunting – in 1874 it was thought that only a single pair remained, with '49ers' finding selling meat more profitable than mining for gold. The most popular source of turtle meat was the giant Galápagos tortoises, imported from the islands. Killing and butchering turtles became a sport known as 'turpining', and this activity was the focus of gambling among the settlers.

In 1851 a newspaper article in the *Daily Alta California* describes the sudden appearance of around a hundred turtles 'perambulating in true turtle style' through the streets of San Francisco.[10] The animals had escaped from the yard of a local restaurant. One of the runaway turtles was spotted 'somersaulting' off the wharf at the foot of Clay Street, and heading for the Farallon Islands. The newspaper reported that the turtle had a smile on his face as he leapt from the pier, seemingly delighted with his escape.

As gold began to become harder to find, money for expensive turtle meat became less available. The turtle trade to San Francisco slowly diminished, before being brought to a close with the

Galápagos tortoise.

South Farallon Island, California
(Landing Cove in Fisherman's Bay.)

The Farallon Islands, c. 1870.

coming of the Civil War and transcontinental railroads. An archaeologist working on turtle bones in the area in the present day noted that the arrival of these historical events likely saved the Galápagos tortoise from extinction.[11]

TURTLE SOUP

Although an unappetizing topic for modern-day turtle enthusiasts, it is impossible to consider the commercial and material use of the turtle without a discussion of turtle soup. First, however, what is turtle soup? Fifty years ago the answer to this question would have been fairly obvious – most cookbooks contained one or more recipes for the dish, and canned turtle soup was readily available in supermarkets. Today, few people in Western countries have eaten turtle. This sharp turnaround in the turtle's fortunes is tied to the developing conservation movement, and the cultural perception of the creature.

Human consumption of turtles has a long history stretching back to prehistoric times. Turtles were hunted, killed and often cooked over a fire by indigenous communities in diverse geographic locations. In more recent times, however, the overwhelming gastronomical fashion for consuming turtles has been in the form of soup. Many of the world's earliest cookbooks contain recipes for turtle soup, with a basic recipe usually involving turtle meat, garlic and onions, assorted vegetables such as celery and tomatoes, and often sherry. Beyond this utilitarian formula, there have been a wide range of regional and cultural variants of the turtle-based broth.

In 1796 the earliest known printed cookbook from North America, *American Cookery*, was published in Hartford, Connecticut. The cookbook's author was Amelia Simmons, about whom very little is known. The book's title pages and cover introduce the author as 'Amelia Simmons, An American Orphan'.[12] *American Cookery*'s turtle soup is one of only two recipes in the book that involve the use of forcemeat (a kind of processed meat combining lean meat with fat), and is considered the book's highest point of elaboration and sophistication.[13] The connection between colonization and cookbooks has been noted for the role played by recipe books in the 'civilizing mission' of European colonists.[14] The cultural influence of cooking, however, flowed in both directions.

Turtle soup began to disappear off menus in the early twentieth century. Overexploitation of the animal for human consumption

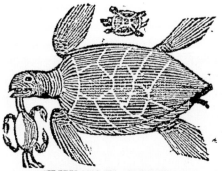

TURTLE SOUP.

THIS DAY and TOMORROW, at ELEVEN o'clock,

A fine SEA TURTLE

will be served up at the PRATT-ST. HOTEL.

Turtle or Terrapin SOUP, and *Soft CRABS*, every day during the season, and private families served as usual. JOHN REDDING.

☞ J. R. is making preparations to accommodate his customers on the 4th *July*, with the greatest delicacies of the season, of which notice will be given. july 1—2t

led to the introduction of several laws in the 1970s to protect species of turtle frequently used in soup, such as alligator snapping turtles, and to ban their commercial harvesting. Further south, turtle harvesting for canned soup in Australia during the early twentieth century led to precipitous declines in the animals' numbers. The short life span of a famed turtle cannery on Heron Island, which opened in 1925, demonstrates the effects on turtle populations of indiscriminate harvesting. As early as 1929, marine biologist F. W. Moorhouse, employed by the Queensland government, expressed concerns about the dwindling turtle numbers around Heron Island.[15] On Moorhouse's recommendation, some prohibitions on turtle harvesting were put in place in 1932, and in the same year, the cannery at Heron Island closed. Increasing alarm over the health of turtle populations, and concerns about the cruelty involved in their mass harvesting, led the Queensland government to make all sea turtles protected species in 1968.[16]

The change of culinary fashions relating to turtles was also guided by increasing public affection for the animals. The popularity of turtle pets grew swiftly in the twentieth century, especially for the red-eared slider turtle. Red-eared sliders originated in the United States and Mexico, but quickly (while moving slowly) spread across the globe.

In Japan, red-eared sliders became popular after the Second World War. The popularity of the species came at the expense of native turtles, which the sliders now vastly outnumber. Indeed, red-eared sliders are considered among the worst international pest animals by the International Union for Conservation of Nature. The influence of the invasive red-eared turtles as pets resulted in a cultural change in how Japanese audiences conceptualized the animals. While toy turtles from the 1920s to the 1950s were painted in the muted browns of native Japanese species, after

Terrapin soup tureen, lid and liner, 1880–90.

93

the 1950s toy turtles became coloured with bright reds, yellows and greens, reflecting the slider turtle.[17]

Also in the mid-twentieth century, turtles became associated with anthropomorphic figures from popular culture. These included Yertle the Turtle, and Bert the Turtle from the *Duck and Cover* instructional films, shown to schoolchildren during the Cold War to inform them how to react to the nuclear threat. The booming popularity of turtles outside the kitchen saw a rapid decrease in their status as a dietary staple.

Although the demand for turtle meat has declined in many areas, the trend is not universal. In the present day, turtles continue to be overexploited and harvested for the food and pet industries, despite numerous legal prohibitions at the national and international levels. A 2014 report by the Indian Ocean Sea Turtle Agreement showed that turtles were being illegally traded to China to be used in food and medicines, and to Japan and Taiwan to produce traditional crafts from their shells. The report found traded turtles were frequently sourced from Indonesia, Malaysia and the Philippines. The modern illegal turtle trade

A red-eared slider turtle.

involves countries from all over the globe, including the United States and India, where the harvesting is having a disastrous effect on indigenous turtle populations.

Turtles are farmed commercially in countries all over the world. Many of these farms are illegal, with turtles being kept in inhumane and unsanitary conditions. In 2018 police in Mallorca raided one of Europe's largest illegal turtle farms. At the farm, they found over 1,000 endangered turtles and more than seven hundred eggs, as well as other threatened species, which were to be sold for €10,000 each.[18] The protected turtles had been smuggled from the United States, Mexico and Canada.

It has become increasingly clear over recent years that it is unwise to eat turtles. Two of the most compelling reasons to abstain from turtle meat relate to environmental factors: while the first reason relates to the welfare of the turtle, the second concerns human health.

Turtles are included on CITES (Convention on International Trade in Endangered Species) endangered list, meaning it is

Green turtle.

illegal to kill turtles (and therefore eating them is off the table). Turtles, as we have seen, are vitally important to environmental health, and large-scale commercial harvesting diminishes and distorts their populations. The human preference for some species of turtle over others means that the decrease in turtle numbers is not uniform, disrupting the balance between species of turtle, and further destabilizing ecosystems.

Second, environmental degradation has seen turtle meat become increasingly rich in pollutants, and in many areas, mercury. The dramatic increase of heavy metals in marine organisms in recent years is related to the broader issue of ocean contamination. The turtles' role in the food chain, combined with their long lives, makes them particularly susceptible to building up heavy stores of environmental pollutants in their bodies. Pollutants such as mercury, DDT, PCBs and Mirex may accumulate in the turtle through its diet. The high levels of these contaminants make turtle consumption extremely hazardous for humans and other turtle predators. In a 2018 study, green turtles from the Pacific Ocean showed higher levels of cadmium in their bodies than dolphins.[19] This finding was surprising, given the dolphins' higher trophic level in the food chain, with green turtles being herbivorous.

There is a further hazard for humans in eating turtles: the consumption of sea turtles can result in chelonitoxism, an often-fatal type of food poisoning. There have been several outbreaks of chelonitoxism in recent years, often linked to the ingestion of hawksbill or green turtles. There is no known antidote for chelonitoxism, meaning prevention through avoiding the consumption of turtles is vital.

The accumulation of hazardous pollutants in turtles' bodies makes them particularly significant for the effective monitoring of the health of marine systems. Turtles are considered a 'sentinel species', reflecting the impact and spread of pollutants through the environment. The high profile of radioactive mutant turtles in popular culture may cause some apprehension around the combination of shelled reptiles and nuclear power – yet turtles have proven excellent allies in monitoring and measuring radioactivity in aquatic systems.[20]

Ecologists at the University of Georgia's Savannah River Ecology Lab use slider turtles to monitor levels of radiation contamination around a nuclear facility. After first happening on a radiated turtle in the laboratory by chance, the scientists have spent years measuring radiation levels in the animals. As well as giving insights into the health of the area around the Savannah River Site, a nuclear fuels production facility, the research assists in directing clean-up efforts from the United States Government.

While turtles are doing their bit for the environment, they have also gained some benefits from their participation. The focused attention on this population of turtles has enhanced the modern understanding of many ecological issues surrounding turtles, such as the long-range terrestrial movements of turtles, how seasonal changes affect the animals' metabolic rates, and the kinetics of radioactive elements.[21]

TORTOISESHELL

The turtle's shell is, in many ways, its defining feature. Through the prehistoric fossil record to pop culture icons, turtles and shells are conceptually fused. The turtle's shell is of crucial value to the creature and a likely cause of its evolutionary success. For humans, however, the turtle's shell has long held a monetary value, one at odds with the vital needs of its owner.

Despite its name, 'tortoiseshell' is most commonly associated with the caraspacial and plastron plates of hawksbill sea turtles. Tortoiseshell has been used as an ornamental gem material since antiquity. In predynastic Egypt, tortoiseshell was fashioned into combs, jewellery and decorative plates.[22] The enormous size of the tortoiseshell trade in the ancient world is evident in textual records from Greece in the first century CE, where tortoiseshell receives more mentions than any other object of trade.[23] Tortoiseshell was used by the ancient Greeks for personal ornamentation, but also for the decoration of furniture.

The use of tortoiseshell veneer continued into more modern times, experiencing a revival in seventeenth-century Europe. The resurgence is generally attributed to the influence of André Charles Boulle, who lent his name to the practice of boulle marquetry. Boulle was the chief cabinetmaker for Louis XIV, and he filled the royal palace at Versailles with his tortoiseshell-covered pieces. Indeed, in the words of antique specialist Christophe Pourny, Boulle 'deployed tortoiseshell *ad nauseam*' on the Baroque French furniture he created for the Sun King.[24]

In Japan, tortoiseshell (called *bekko*, thought to originate from the words for 'turtle' and 'armour') was used for thousands of years, with the shell being polished and crafted into brooches, necklaces, eyeglass frames and delicate works of art.[25] Turtles gave their names (but happily, not their shells) to another traditional item of clothing, *kikkō*, a type of armour made from leather, with the armour's hexagonal patterning and toughness considered reminiscent of turtle shells.

While frequently decorative, tortoiseshell could also have divine uses. In the Shang and Zhou dynasties of ancient China, tortoiseshell fragments inscribed with pictographic writing were called 'oracle bones' and used in the process of communicating with deities. These ancient oracle bones, some over 3,500 years old, preserve some of the earliest examples of Chinese writing. The turtles' shells would be heated, causing them to crack in all directions, and the diviner would interpret the directions and types of cracks as divine messages.

Turtle shells were also used in ancient Chinese medicine, notably in *guilinggao* (turtle jelly), a gluelike substance made by boiling the shells of turtles, believed to be beneficial for human kidneys. The animal's blood has been considered in traditional medicine to be a tonic for improving health. In 1993 Chinese athletes training with controversial coach Ma Junren for track events at the Olympics credited their fast times to drinking the blood of turtles. Despite these claims, several of Ma's athletes

Brass-and-tortoiseshell marquetry adorns a commode by André Charles Boulle (Paris, 1642–1732).

Underside of a turtle's shell from the Shang Dynasty, prepared with inscription for divine communication.

were later dropped from China's team before the 2000 Olympics because of concerns involving illegal doping.[26]

The popular use of tortoiseshell in furnishings and other decorative items was driven by the perceived attractiveness of the mottled material and its durability. The fashion for ornamental tortoiseshell took a great toll on populations of the animals, comparable to the disastrous effects of the ivory trade on elephants. In 1973 an 80 per cent decline in the number of hawksbill sea turtles recorded in ocean basins from several countries saw trading in tortoiseshell banned internationally. The appearance of tortoiseshell is instead mimicked by artificial substitutes, often made from plastics.

Chinese medicinal jellied turtle soup (*guilinggao*).

TURTLES AND TECHNOLOGY

The turtle has adapted to suit a composite world. The animal's
wide-ranging geographic span, however, has long involved one
important limitation – despite their many impressive qualities,
turtles cannot fly. Or can they? While not known for their aero-
dynamic qualities, turtles have had several notable forays into the
skies, most intriguingly in the form of animal astronauts.

On 14 September 1968, the Soviet spacecraft *Zond 5* was fired
into orbit. Although 'unmanned', the craft carried a motley animal

Russian *Zond 5* stamp, 1969.

crew of space pioneers, including the two tortoises, some flies, mealworms, bacteria and plant matter. On 18 September, *Zond 5* flew around the Moon, making it the first spacecraft to circle the Moon and return to Earth, and turtles among the very first earthlings to circumnavigate the Moon, and see the Sun rising over our home planet.

Interactions between turtles and humans took a new turn in 2013, with the first remote-controlled turtle animals being developed in Korea, using non-invasive technology. Turtles were chosen for the experiment because of two features fundamental to their image – their slow movements, and their ability to navigate land and water environments. The successful control of the turtles has possible applications for espionage and (very slow) search-and-rescue projects in the future.

As well as taking the first tiny steps for turtles and a giant leap for earthlings, turtles have further experience with aviation closer to home. In December 2018, 32 Kemp's ridley sea turtles from New England in the United States were reported to have 'flown south for the winter'.[27] The turtles had had to be rescued in the waters around Cape Cod after being 'cold stunned', a condition similar to hypothermia. Volunteer pilots ferried their flippered cargo to Florida, where they could recover in balmier weather.

SPORTING TURTLES

Turtles and racing have a modern connection, beyond the familiar metaphor of the tortoise and the hare. In the sport of turtle racing, the field is entirely made up of turtles. The animal athletes are generally placed in the centre of a circle on level ground, and once the race has started, they compete to see who can reach the outside of the circle first. Turtle racing has a long and colourful history,

with close ties to gambling. The sport is thought to have roots in the Caribbean, and from there spread to the United States.

Turtle racing has numerous fans, but it has not always been popular with the law, and has been connected with organized crime. In 1930 Al Capone decided to expand his gambling empire to include turtle racing. The notorious gangster had been released from prison in March of that year, and was considered to be the number one 'Public Enemy' on the list of the Chicago Crime Commission. This followed an attack on George Moran's rival gang at a North Side garage on 14 February 1929, which led to the deaths of seven men (widely known as the 'Valentine's Day massacre').

Capone is widely credited with bringing greyhound racing to Chicago, and like fellow gangsters Lucky Luciano and Bugsy Siegel, he was heavily invested in racing dogs around Illinois and Florida. Having amassed great profits from his dog-racing enterprises, Capone was enthusiastic about the idea of bringing the sport of turtle racing to Chicago. The relatively small size of the reptilian racers was particularly appealing to the gangster. Chicago in 1930 was under the laws of the Prohibition era, meaning the sale of alcohol was illegal in the city. Capone's plan was to build tiny racetracks in the thousands of speakeasies he ran throughout the state of Illinois, where his liquor was sold and money could be made from betting on the turtle races.

Capone dispatched an aide to Ponca City in Oklahoma, where he bought 5,000 mud turtles for the new business. A newspaper report in the *Baltimore Sun* of 7 November 1930 commented that Capone didn't adequately research his new venture, which led to its failure. According to the newspaper report, turtle racing at the time involved setting up each turtle on a miniature, narrow track, where the animal could not turn around. The secret to the race was that the starting point beneath the turtles was made uncomfortably hot, forcing the turtles along the track in search of a cooler place to rest. Capone's aide overlooked the need for separate, neatly divided runways for the competitors, instead setting up a single hot spot for all the turtles. When the grand test was conducted, the design of the course was found to make racing impossible: 'the turtles headed in all directions dodging the heat and tangled up each other.'

Capone was furious at the failure of his turtle racing business, having found himself with a herd of 5,000 turtles and nowhere for them to run. In a hurry to return to Florida, the gangster decided to cut his losses, and ordered his henchmen to dump the racing turtles at any place they could find. The henchmen set the animals loose in the city of Chicago. On 2 November 1930, 2,000 of the mud turtles were discovered wandering down South Michigan Avenue. The remaining 3,000 animals were found later the same week, meandering around a vacant lot in the suburb of Cicero – an area synonymous with Capone.

With their sporting careers reaching an untimely end, the 'orphans' were gathered up by the Illinois Humane Society. The newspaper's account of the incident ends on a rather alarming note, reporting that the secretary of the Humane Society, a Dr George A. Scott, had publicly declared his intention to raise the issue of the turtles' mistreatment with Capone when he returned to Chicago. Capone's abandoned turtles were turned over by the Society to Dr Karl Patterson Schmidt, a noted herpetologist and curator of the Field Museum. The failure of Capone's attempt to bring turtle racing to Chicago in 1930 may have prevented the sport from becoming stigmatized by the connection to organized crime – as was the case with the sport of dog-racing in the 1930s, 1940s and 1950s.

UNLEASHING THE TURTLES OF WAR

Turtles in modern culture are often portrayed as peaceful ocean-goers, but their sturdy shells have provided inspiration for human combatants in many historical conflicts. In Mesoamerica, the Spanish conquistador Bernal Díaz del Castillo reported sailing along the coast of the New World and seeing warriors holding shields made of carefully polished turtle shells. The turtle's physical form is referenced in the Roman battle formation, the *testudo* ('tortoise'), which involved aligning the soldiers' shields to create a protective barrier.

Usually, animals closely associated with military symbolism are predators with a reputation for ferocity – a warrior may be said to fight like a lion, or to be as fierce as a tiger. Yet the turtle appears prominently in many of the most famous conflicts of the last few hundred years, in the continuation of an ancient trend with a likely genesis in the animal's natural stoicism, its protective 'armour' and its capacity for endurance.

The turtle's shape and protective shell have seen it used as a muse by designers of military craft. The world's first armoured boat, the Korean *Geobukseon*, was called the 'Turtle Ship', due to its resemblance to a turtle.[28] It was built around 1540 CE, and designed by the well-known Korean admiral Yi Sun-Shin. Unlike the animal for which the Turtle Ship was named, the *Geobukseon* was developed to move with great speed, as well as being structurally sturdy.[29] Cannons were fired through the mouth of a dragon carved into the ship's bow, and a turtle's tail, armed with gunports, was attached to the stern of the craft.[30]

The turtle lent its name and form to another pioneering sea vessel – the first submarine. The first known submersible craft with documented use in combat is the *American Turtle*, created by David Bushnell in 1775 for use in the American Revolutionary War. On 6 September 1776 the *American Turtle* was deployed to her only combat mission. The plan was to use the submersible craft to get close to the British Navy anchored in New York Harbor, and to affix mines to HMS *Eagle*, the fleet's flagship, and destroy it. Efforts at attaching the mine to the British ship failed, due to a

Reconstructed Korean *Geobukseon* boat.

lack of adequate upward buoyant pressure to enable the mine to
be screwed into place. After several attempts, the mission was
aborted, and the *Turtle* floated away downstream.

The craft left a lasting impression on maritime history and
upon the Revolutionary War's participants. *Turtle* was discussed
in letters exchanged between George Washington and Thomas
Jefferson. In a letter to Jefferson dated 26 September 1785 –
shortly before becoming the first president of the United States
– Washington described the submarine as 'an effort of genius'.[31]

The turtle's physical appearance, and its mythical connection
to warfare, have seen it provide inspiration for many military
innovations. The animal's placid nature, however, has seen it
make a meaningful contribution on many battlefields as a companion to human combatants. In 1940 Australian troops training
in Palestine were accompanied by a turtle named 'Tim'. As the
mascot for the 2/2nd Battalion, Tim (thought to be a spur-
thighed tortoise) helped the morale of troops working a long way
from their homes. Tim's unit went on to play a significant role in

Captain D. Michelson with a turtle named Tim: the mascot of the 2/2nd Battalion.

numerous conflicts during the Second World War, but his fate is unknown.

During the Gallipoli campaign of the First World War, a turtle's friendship provided comfort to a New Zealand soldier. Thomas O'Connor was guarding his trench by night when a turtle fell over the edge and almost landed on top of him. O'Connor recovered from his shock at the turtle's sudden entrance, and saw that it was struggling to make its way back out of the trench – so he built a little ramp to help the animal on its way. To the soldier's surprise, the turtle returned later that night, and began to make regular visits, giving the soldier great companionship. Sadly, while O'Connor was away fulfilling his duties as a stretcher-bearer, another group of troops occupied the trench and killed the turtle for soup. O'Connor was so distressed at the death of his friend that he rescued the animal's shell, and carried it with him for the rest of the war.[32] The shell now rests in New Zealand's National Army Museum, where it stands as a memorial to a cross-species friendship between a human and a turtle during a terrible time of conflict.

Through its involvement in human trade and technology, the intrepid turtle has survived continuous harvesting for meat, jewellery, medicine and many other materials. Yet the story of turtles in trade and technology is one that tells as much about human history as it does about the turtles. Considering turtles in trade and technology serves as a reminder of the many ways that human ingenuity and ambition have been served by our turtle

Hatchling sea turtles on the beach in Aruba in the Dutch Antilles.

friends, and of the perpetual balancing act between living creatures and the environment.

Conservation is often thought of as a modern trend, but its history stretches back hundreds of years. At many points in the past, concerned and far-seeing individuals and groups have taken steps to preserve the natural wonder that is the turtle – from legislators in seventeenth-century Bermuda to members of the Illinois Humane Society in Prohibition-era Chicago. Concern for the preservation of turtles lies at the heart of some of the earliest pieces of conservation legislation, giving added weight to the half-shelled reptiles in their modern incarnation as eco-warriors.

5 Modern Art and Literature

Come now my heavenly tortoiseshell,
and become a speaking instrument.
Sappho

Turtles have fuelled the human imagination for millennia. As with turtle myths and legends, modern literary incarnations of the animals are linked to the creation and order of the earth and the state of the natural world. The essayist Henry David Thoreau mused at length on the 'irresistible necessity for mud turtles', which causes 'Nature' to tenaciously overcome all hurdles that would prevent their existence. The focus on turtles and environmental concerns can also be seen in the Pulitzer-Prize-winning book *Turtle Island* (1974), by beat poet and essayist Gary Snyder.

Turtles and children would appear at first glance to have little common ground, but an appreciation for the quiet and languid animals can be found in numerous works of literature for young audiences. The turtle's ancient origins and its physical distinctiveness are artistically connected to qualities of wisdom and stability, but the appearance of the odd melancholy turtle in literature perhaps warns that an oversupply of slowness may lead to stagnation.

Rather than giving cause for disqualification, the turtle's ungainly and slow movements, and its distinctive physicality, have provided motivation for poetic appraisals. Even many scientists – a breed better known for verbal economy than pleasing turns of phrase – show unexpected gestures towards capturing the turtle with well-chosen words. The conservationist Carl Safina described turtles as being 'angels of the deep – ancient, ageless, great-grandparents of the world'.[1] The well-known scientific journal for turtle studies *Chelonian Conservation and Biology* devotes its final section to turtle poetry. Many notable poets have had their works included in the journal's poetry section, including recently the late Chilean poet Pablo Neruda. Neruda's poem 'La Tortuga' presents an account of the life of a turtle, following the animal's movements through the water and its time under the sun, before finally becoming rocklike and sleeping.

The American poet Ogden Nash wrote two poems on turtles. The first lauded the challenges involved in turtles' mating while living 'twixt plated decks'.[2] In a later work, Nash considered the difficulty of discriminating among different types of turtles. The poet expressed his confusion neatly by conflating the names of the animals, stating, 'I know the turtoise is a tortle.'[3]

John William Godward, *The Quiet Pet*, 1906, oil on canvas.

A sympathetic piece on the turtle was composed by the Pulitzer-Prize-winning American poet Kay Ryan in 1994.[4] Ryan begins the poem 'Turtle' with a clear statement on the poem's subject – the poet asks the rhetorical question of why anyone, given the choice, would be a turtle. Many of the problems encountered by the turtle that are identified by the poet relate to mobility: the animal's lack of grace on terrestrial surfaces is noted, and the frequent risk of getting stuck with limited manoeuvrability to free itself. The poem ends noting the patience of the turtle, seemingly tolerant of its difficult and at times inelegant position in life, and its acceptance of its meagre stature.

The human and animal connection was a focus of the work of Mexican poet José Emilio Pacheco. As part of a broader rumination on the difficulties of cross-species interactions, Pacheco wrote of the problems that develop from a lack of human insight into the qualities of the turtle. Pacheco's poem 'The Well', published in 1993, notes an ancient tradition of keeping a turtle at the bottom of a well to purify the water. Pacheco observes that the

Paolo Porpora, *Still-life with a Snake, Frogs, Tortoise and Lizard*, mid-17th century, oil on canvas.

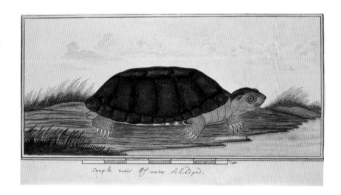

presence of the turtle in the well has the opposite of its intended
effect, contaminating the water supply. The turtle in the well illustrates a common theme in Pacheco's work – the need to respect
animals for their inherent worth, and to guard against human
pretensions of omnipotence.[5]

Turtles are poetically described in Russell Hoban's novel *Turtle
Diary* (1975). The turtles of London Zoo are described as holding
'thousands of miles in their speechless eyes, submarine skies in
their flipper-wings'. The captive turtles function in the story as a
kind of totem for the human protagonists, who are isolated by
their loneliness. The pair are inspired by the animals' uncanny
ability to find their way home, and they work together to return
the turtles to the sea. The novel was made into a critically acclaimed
movie in 1985, and in both versions the release of the turtles
assists in transforming the lives of their rescuers. In this way, the
story of *Turtle Diary* reflects a tradition seen in parts of Indonesia,
where captive turtles are released into the wild to bring blessings
and good fortune to the community.

Human and turtle interactions also feature in the work of
Ernest Hemingway. Turtle hunting, or 'turtling', is described in
the novel *The Old Man and the Sea*. Published in 1952, the

Pulitzer-Prize-winning book tells the story of an old Cuban fisherman named Santiago. In the story, the activity of hunting turtles at sea is said to ruin one's eyesight, due to the need to stare at the sparkling surface of the ocean for long spans of time, waiting to spot a turtle. The book's protagonist, Santiago, has good vision despite years of turtling, likely due to his use of remora fish to locate the turtles. The use of innovative techniques in fishing, and the unusual perseverance of Santiago's vision, sets him apart from other characters, while grounding the novel in its Cuban setting.[6]

Turtles and Pulitzer-Prize-winning novels are combined in Gary Snyder's *Turtle Island*, published in 1974. In the book's introduction, Snyder explains that the volume takes its name from the Native American name for North America, as well as from the 'idea found world-wide, of the earth, or cosmos even, sustained by a great turtle or serpent-of-eternity'.[7] In this way, the title of *Turtle Island* reflects the ecological focus of the book, which invites

Loggerhead sea turtle with outstretched flippers.

readers to consider how humans need to live in greater harmony with nature.

The cosmic turtle, featured in the title of Snyder's work, appears in Terry Pratchett's *Discworld* series. The cosmic turtle, A'Tuin the Great, is introduced in the first book of the fantasy series, *The Colour of Magic* (1983). A'Tuin belongs to the fictional turtle species of *Chelys galactica*, and it carries the land of Discworld on its back. As in Hindu mythology, the planet rests on the back of four elephants who stand on the back of the turtle. The introduction of the cosmic turtle is accompanied by the author's consideration of its origins:

> There was the theory that A'Tuin had come from nowhere and would continue at a uniform crawl, or steady gait, into nowhere, for all time. This theory was popular among academics.
>
> An alternative, favoured by those of a religious persuasion, was that A'Tuin was crawling from the Birthplace

Glenda Jackson and Ben Kingsley in the 1985 film *Turtle Diary*.

Painted rawhide shield with turtle symbol, Plains Peoples, North America, pre-1825.

to the Time of Mating, as were all the stars in the sky which were, obviously, also carried by giant turtles. When they arrived they would briefly and passionately mate, for the first and only time, and from that fiery union new turtles would be born to carry a new pattern of worlds. This was known as the Big Bang hypothesis.[8]

In the second book of the series, *The Light Fantastic* (1986), it is revealed that wizards have been studying to get an insight into A'Tuin's thoughts. The wizards are said to have 'trained up on tortoises and giant sea turtles first, to get the hang of the chelonian frame of mind', before attempting to read the cosmic turtle's mind.[9] Pratchett plays upon the longevity and languid pace of the turtle animal – the author describes A'Tuin's mind as extremely

Turtle fresco by the Italian Mannerist painter Lorenzo Sabbatini (c. 1530–1576).

Frederick S. Church, 'Brer Fox Tackles Brer Tarrypin', from Joel Chandler Harris's *Uncle Remus, His Songs and His Sayings: The Folk-lore of the Old Plantation* (1881).

vast, but also incredibly slow-moving, frustrating the wizards in their efforts at mind-reading.

Children and turtles seem to induce a natural sympathy. While not by some standards 'cute', and not especially cuddly, turtles are rarely aggressive, and are easy for children to keep up with. Turtles turn up frequently in books directed to audiences of children of all ages. Turtles and terrapins feature in the famous stories of Brer Rabbit. These stories, while well known, are difficult to precisely categorize, but likely originated in oral storytelling traditions with roots in African and Cherokee cultures. The stories were collected by the American folklorist Joel Chandler Harris, who wrote and published the Brer Rabbit stories as a set of tales told by the fictional character Uncle Remus. *The Complete Tales of Uncle Remus* features several turtle-based characters, including Mr Mud Turtle,

Brer Tarrypin and Miss Tarrypin, and touch on the long-running competition between turtles and hares. While all three characters are friends of the protagonist rabbit, Brer Tarrypin is at times able to beat Brer Rabbit in competition, with the help of his wife, Miss Tarrypin.

Theodore Seuss Geisel is better known by the pen name 'Dr Seuss'. In recent years, Seuss has become recognized as one of the most influential poets in America, whose work has changed the usage of the English language and added new words to popular vernacular.[10] Throughout his oeuvre, Seuss shows a fascination with animals, real and imaginary, resulting in some of the most enduring characters of children's picture books. Before the publication of his well-known story *The Cat in the Hat*, Seuss used a turtle as his obnoxious protagonist in the classic children's book *Yertle the Turtle*. The eponymous turtle is introduced as the 'king of the pond', on the far-away island of Sala-ma-Sond. The rhyming couplet of the turtle's watery home with the fictional name of the island is typical of Dr Seuss's poetic style. Despite its humorous narrative, *Yertle the Turtle* was inspired by Seuss's opposition to fascism and authoritarian rule during and following the Second World War. The eponymous Yertle was intended to satirize Adolf Hitler, early drawings for the book showing the turtle wearing the dictator's distinctive moustache.[11]

Seuss's illustrations for *Yertle* include a tower of turtles – a creative repurposing of the popular 'turtles all the way down' motif. The tower of turtles was used by Seuss in 1942, around a decade prior to his publication of *Yertle*, in an editorial cartoon for the New York City paper *PM*. The cartoon showed a tower of turtles forming an awkward 'v' shape, with the caption sharply noting that 'You can't build a substantial "v" out of turtles!' The turtle at the bottom of the tower (the furthest way down) is somewhat unsubtly labelled 'Dawdling producers'. The imagery of a turtle drawing its head into its shell and isolating itself from trouble had a wide currency in the late nineteenth and early twentieth century.

In the children's story, the tower of turtles is formed under the orders of the tyrannical king of turtles, Yertle, who wishes to rule over the whole earth. Yertle orders increasingly large numbers of turtles to stand on top of one another, so that he may sit atop them and reign over all he sees. Despite the turtles' complaints, Yertle insists on obedience. Finally, one of the turtles at the bottom of the tower gives a deliberately loud burp, shaking the king's tower and causing him to fall with a 'plunk!' into the mud. The turtles are liberated, and Seuss ends the story on an optimistic note:

And the turtles, of course . . . all the turtles are free
As turtles and, maybe, all creatures should be.[12]

In 1979 the German children's author Michael Ende wrote *Die undendliche Geschichte*, about a boy, Bastian Balthazar Bux, who reads a magical book which transports him to a land of fantasy. The book was published in English as *The Neverending Story* in 1982, and is generally considered to be a modern classic of children's literature. The story is often noted as an example of the German *Bildungsroman* tradition, a literary genre involving the education or moral development of the protagonist.[13]

A popular film of the book in 1984 brought many of the vivid characters from the book to life, using 'hand-made magic', in the period prior to the dominance of computer-generated images in special effects.[14] These characters, portrayed by a number of puppeteers, include the Luck Dragon Falkor, the 'creature of dark-ness' Gmork, and Morla, the Aged One, a giant turtle. Ende's chelid character is notable for the author's subversive use of tra-ditional turtle tropes. The common cultural image of the turtle as a wise and long-lived creature is distorted in *The Neverending Story*, with Morla presenting a shadow side to this mythic archetype.

Morla's longevity makes her knowledgeable but world-weary. The turtle's jaded perspective makes her reluctant to assist Atreyu, the story's child warrior protagonist. She is described as having 'empty-gazing eyes', and her demeanour is melancholic and contrary. Morla attributes her own apathy to extreme longevity, telling the warrior that 'nothing matters'. Morla's age is further emphasized in her slow and lethargic demeanour, her epithet and her reaction to youthful Atreyu. Despite Morla's vast knowledge, Atreyu outwits her into divulging the information he requires for his quest. He argues that if the turtle truly believed that nothing mattered, she would be less resistant to answering his questions. Morla concedes the point, revealing that it is likely a question of personality rather than age causing her recalcitrant attitude.

An old turtle is featured in the children's picture book *The Three Questions*, by Jon J. Muth. In this volume, however, the wise turtle in question is portrayed positively. *The Three Questions* is based on a short story written in 1885 by Leo Tolstoy. The original

Desert tortoise (*Gopherus agassizii*) drinking from a roadway in Joshua Tree National Park, California.

story was a fable about a Russian tsar who asks a hermit for the answer to three philosophical questions: 'when is the most important time?', 'who is the most necessary person?' and 'what is the most important affair?'

In Muth's picture book, the human actors of Tolstoy's story are mostly replaced by animals, with a little boy taking the place of the tsar. The answer to the titular three questions is given by a kindly turtle, who replaces the character of the hermit from the fable. The hermit, like the turtle, is presented as old – he is frail, and requires help with his digging in the garden. The choice of a turtle by Muth shows nice interplay with the animal's reputation for burrowing in the ground. The turtle's name in the story is Leo, in deference to the fable's original author. Leo the turtle is presented inhabiting familiar qualities for a literary chelid. He is slow, wise, benevolent and patient. He is also generous in sharing his home and knowledge – in contrast to Ende's miserable Morla. The fact that it is Leo the turtle who gives the answers to the eponymous three questions conveys the importance of mindful presence in the current moment.[15] Muth's choice of a turtle for the character of Leo gives the figure credibility, through his artistic engagement with common turtle tropes.

While not strictly involving a turtle, the story of *Alice's Adventures in Wonderland* features a turtle-like creature that reflects the surreal quality and dark humour of the narrative. The book was written by the English author Charles Lutwidge Dodgson under the pseudonym Lewis Carroll, with original illustrations by John Tenniel. The book was published in 1865. The story's heroine, Alice, encounters the Mock Turtle while travelling through a fantastical land she discovers after falling down a rabbit hole.

The Mock Turtle is a tragic creature, with tear-filled eyes that inspire instant sympathy in Alice (but not in the Griffin accompanying her, who comments that the creature's misery is 'all his

John Tenniel's
original 1865
illustration for
Lewis Carroll's
*Alice's Adventures in
Wonderland.* Alice
sitting between
the Gryphon and
the Mock Turtle.

John Tenniel's original 1865 illustration for Lewis Carroll's *Alice's Adventures in Wonderland.* Alice sitting between the Gryphon and the Mock Turtle.

fancy').[16] The creature's appearance is a visual pun on the popular Victorian soup, used as a cheap substitute for authentic turtle soup. Mock turtle soup is made using offal, such as calves' brains or hooves, as the gelatinous meat of the soup. The mixed quality of mock turtle soup is reflected in the book's original illustrations by Tenniel, who draws the character with the body and front flippers of a sea turtle, but with the head and hind feet of a calf. Drawing on his turtle background, the Mock Turtle instructs Alice on the nature of life under the sea, and the surreal scene ends with him singing a song about turtle soup.

As well as providing inspiration for written works, the turtle has lent its form to numerous pieces in the visual arts. In early Christian art, the turtle is at times presented as a symbol of sin and darkness, and contrasted against a cock representing watchfulness and light. St Jerome described the tortoise as 'heretical' for its tendency to dwell in lowly and dirty areas.[17] At other times in Christian symbolism, turtles could depict chastity or reticence. Sea turtles are a religious symbol in Sufism, a branch of Islam. The journey of newly hatched turtles to the sea is believed to represent the human voyage of returning to God.[18]

Perhaps the best-known artwork featuring a turtle from recent times is Henri Matisse's *Bathers with a Turtle*. The painting, composed in 1908, shows a similar composition and subject to the work *Bather by a River* (1909–16), also by Matisse. It is thought that the artist produced the work in response to Picasso's *Three Women* (1908), a work noted for its mythological overtones that subtly reference classical themes of three female figures, such as the Graces.[19] Numerous classical myths have been suggested by scholars as the inspiration for *Bathers*. The painting is considered to subtly reference myths of Aphrodite, but it has been suggested that the artist may be evoking the lesser-known myth of the Arcadian turtle nymph, Chelone.[20] Picasso himself was not immune to the appeal of turtles – the artist owned a pet tortoise from around 1909. The animal was said to wander around his studio, along with cats, dogs and a monkey, and provided the artist with companionship and inspiration.[21] Both paintings show an emphasis on figures within a landscape. The turtle in Matisse's painting is the object of the gaze of the three bathers as well as that of the artist. While the three figures are presented quite sombrely, the turtle shows a surprising energy, stretching for a leaf offered by one of the bathers.

Bathers with a Turtle was purchased in 1908 for the Folkwang Museum in Hagen, Germany. On 24 August 1937, *Bathers with a Turtle* was among numerous works confiscated by the Nazis. The seizure was a result of the Nazi Party's efforts to destroy or confiscate artistic works considered non-traditional, which they described as 'Degenerate Art', or *entartete Kunst*. Hitler himself had once held ambitions of being a professional artist – prior to his political career, Hitler painted many works in a traditional style, but failed to secure a place in an art school.

Part of the movement against modern art was a travelling exhibition called *Degenerate Art* in 1937, followed by the burning and auctioning of confiscated modern artworks in 1939. *Bathers with a Turtle* was sold at the auction of Degenerate Art in 1939. Although condemned as 'garbage' by the Nazi regime, the auctioned pieces were considered 'internationally exploitable'. The painting was bought by Joseph Pulitzer Jr, grandson of the famous newsman Joseph Pulitzer, with the purchase made on Pulitzer Jr's behalf by Pierre Matisse, the artist's son. Pulitzer Jr was known for his exceptional collection of modern art, and for gifting artworks to public institutions. The Pulitzers donated *Bathers with a Turtle* to the St Louis Art Museum in 1964.

In a 1978 interview, Pulitzer Jr recalled the circumstances around the purchase of *Bathers with a Turtle*:

This art was considered degenerate by the German government of that time. It became quite obvious when one looked at the things that they were the most creative works of then-existing artists of that period. So I was able to make arrangements through Pierre Matisse . . . he and I agreed that the Bathers, which I immediately was tremendously impressed by, would be a wonderful thing to try to get . . .[22]

Even members of the Nazi Party could not escape the impact of the artistic purging of the 1930s. Despite his Nazi Party membership, the work of German-Danish watercolourist Emil Nolde was officially condemned by the regime. Nolde was a member of the German art group Die Brücke (The Bridge), who played a role in the development of the Expressionist movement. Die Brücke artists were known for their simplified style and interest in 'primitive' subject-matters.

Nolde enthusiastically embraced National Socialism, promoted darkly anti-Semitic views and enjoyed the patronage of Heinrich Himmler.[23] In 1937, 1,052 of Nolde's artworks were denounced as 'degenerate' and confiscated from museums and galleries. Among his confiscated works was *Swimming Turtle*, a watercolour painted in 1923–4. The artist was further forbidden from engaging in any professional art activities, including buying artistic materials, such as paintbrushes.

In an Orientalist painting by Osman Hamdi Bey, turtles tread a thoughtful line between animality and art. *The Tortoise Trainer*, an oil on canvas from the early twentieth century, shows the artist in the appearance of a dervish. At his feet are a small group of tortoises, feeding on green plants, within the chambers of Bursa's Yeşil Camii (Green Mosque). The artist holds a *ney* flute and a *nakkare* (a type of kettledrum), suggesting a subtle approach to his work with the tortoises, and touching upon the ancient link between turtles and music.[24]

For an ancient creature, turtles have had a surprisingly broad appeal for creators of modern art. Turtles narrowly escaped featuring in the Surrealist art of Salvador Dalí. In his 1942 autobiography, *The Secret Life of Salvador Dalí*, the artist drew a picture of his famous lobster telephone, and included a short essay on his desire to see telephones presented in a range of unusual settings. These settings, often relating to themes of mortality and excess, included the sadistic idea of screwing a telephone to the back of a live turtle.[25]

Vicente do Rego Monteiro, the Brazilian artist known for his contribution to the development of Brazilian Modernism, created *Cat and Turtle* in 1925. The oil painting depicts a cat and turtle pictured in profile, moving alongside one another. The turtle, with its small flippers, keeps a wary eye on the cat, which returns its gaze. The cat's tail is high and rounded, suggesting a playful mood, and the curve of the tail is mirrored in the arched lines of the turtle's shell, the cat's back and the foliage of a potted plant, framing part of the scene. It has been suggested that the curved form of the cat in the picture may be intended to evoke Matisse's rounded bather from *Bathers with a Turtle*. Monteiro may have viewed the painting in a monograph by the Paris-based art historian Adolphe Basler, published in 1924.[26]

Turtles have also been a subject in the Pop art movement, receiving their 'fifteen minutes of fame' in the work of Andy Warhol. Famed for his witty engagement with the cultural icons of modernity, Warhol's lifelong love of animals, and his environmental activism, are less widely known aspects of his identity. The artist's concern for the natural world can be traced throughout his career, even to his legacy following his sudden and untimely death in 1987.

A particular concern for Warhol, with great resonance for turtles, was the issue of beach erosion. Warhol owned a beachfront property in the ecologically significant Montauk Moorlands, on Long Island. Warhol's 6-ha (15 ac.) beach was donated to the Nature Conservancy in 1992, and has become the Andy Warhol Preserve, part of a 970-ha (2,400 ac.) protected area. The area is home to some extremely rare animals, such as the bog copper butterfly, blue spotted salamander, the eastern hognose snake and the spotted turtle.

Osman Hamdi Bey,
The Turtle Trainer,
1906, oil on canvas.

In 1983, twenty years after the emergence of Pop art, Warhol created a series of silkscreen prints called *Endangered Species*. This series featured an African rhinoceros, an elephant, a San Francisco silverspot butterfly and a sea turtle, among others, all luminously realized in Warhol's vivid style.

The distinctive design of the turtle has also provided inspiration for works of sculpture. Albert Laessle produced a number of images of turtles in the early twentieth century. The American sculptor's remarkably detailed and biologically accurate images of animals led to his being described as an 'Animalier' – one of a group of American artists known for their depictions of animals. Laessle's interest in turtles was apparently stimulated by meeting one while in art class. A snapping turtle brought by a colleague for dinner was requisitioned for further study by Laessle. The artist's realistic style likely grew from his appreciation and close observation of live animals, as he is known to have said, 'To do anything with animals, you have to know your subject. Looking at it from the safe side of iron bars won't give you much information.'

Fourth-century turtle-and-cock mosaic at Aquileia Basilica in Friuli, Italy.

Laessle's approach proved greatly effective – indeed, almost too effective. In 1901 Laessle's sculpture *Turtle and Crab* was in contention for the gold medal at the Philadelphia Club. Critics thought the piece too lifelike to be a genuine sculpture, and accused Laessle of casting the work. In response, Laessle created another turtle sculpture, this time using wax, which could not be cast and proving his artistic expertise. A similar story is told of Laessle's remarkably lifelike bronze sculpture *Turning Turtle*, which was shown at the Paris Salon in 1907.

In modern art and literature, turtles show an intimate connection to their natural environment, which has been part of their image from antiquity. In artistic works, turtles often provide a point of contrast with humans and our at-times unharmonious connection to the natural environment.

Turtles, it has been observed, do things differently. From keeping their shoulder girdles inside their ribcages, to laying eggs, turtles have responded to the challenges presented by earth's biosphere in ways that are quite distinct from humans – yet their adaptations have proved enduringly successful. In this way, turtles continually inspire the consideration of new perspectives, and provide a charismatic model for the benefits of adapting ourselves astutely to the world around us.

6 Turtle Power: Popular Culture and Turtles

Slow and steady wins the race.
Aesop

Turtles feature prominently in children's entertainment, due to their charismatic appeal and 'gentle' image.[1] The biological distinctiveness of the animal is often a prominent part of its fictional characterization, but the natural realities of the chelid's physicality are frequently embellished – or entirely superseded – for creative purposes.

Turtles in books, films and television shows aimed at young audiences are often presented in a lighthearted or humorous manner. Beneath the placid surface, however, even two-dimensional turtles in children's entertainment can hold surprising depth. Turtle characters in children's entertainment have a serious job to do in presenting weighty issues in a non-threatening way. Climate change concerns are highlighted in works for young audiences involving turtles, playing upon the creature's close ties to conservation. Turtle characters address social issues such as loneliness and peer pressure – even the threat of thermonuclear war.

TURTLES ON TV

Turtles feature as cartoon characters in numerous television shows for young audiences. The cartoon figures of Franklin the Turtle, Touché Turtle and Cecil the Turtle all draw upon popular

Turtle tattoo.

turtle imagery in different ways. While the turtle animal's physical features and mythic associations are referenced, cartoon turtles often blend fiction and fact. The frequently seen ability of cartoon turtles to remove their shells without harm has no basis in biological reality: the shell is a living part of the animal. The perpetuation of this myth is an exception to the broader creative trend of fictional turtles drawing upon authentic features of the biological animal. In children's entertainment, the removal of the shell means the turtle appears 'naked', vulnerable and a little foolish – it is literally stripped of the protective layer defining its identity.

MANHATTAN THEATRE

F. ZIEGFELD Jr's
PRODUCTION

33RD ST.
AND
BROADWAY.

BRADY & ZIEGFELD
Managers.

THE TURTLE

"I'M NOT SO SLOW."

For children, the turtle's inner vulnerability, hidden beneath a protective facade, may be relatable while navigating the process of socialization.

Franklin is the protagonist of the *Franklin the Turtle* books, written by Brenda Clark and Paulette Bourgeois, and a related Canadian television series. Franklin's characterization emphasizes the connection between turtles and children: he is portrayed as a child of six, and encounters common childhood problems, such as the need to learn to share with others (*Franklin and Harriet*). Franklin is presented anthropomorphically, but his adventures sometimes relate specifically to his identity as a chelid. In *Franklin and the Dark*, Franklin is too afraid of the dark to enter his own shell. Instead, he drags his carapace behind him on a rope.

Another cartoon turtle is Touché Turtle. Touché is a gallant, fencing turtle who battles evil with his sheepdog sidekick in *The New Hanna-Barbera Cartoon Series* (1962). Touché carries a sword, and his shell is used as an impromptu telephone box, into which he retreats to receive incoming calls for his help. Touché Turtle demonstrates the exceptional flexibility of the hero-turtle motif.

The story of the tortoise and the hare has had many adaptations in modern popular culture, including in the labyrinthine cartoon universe of Looney Tunes. Cecil the Turtle's appearance in the Looney Tunes cartoons highlights the animal's slow gait, and his reputation for cleverness. Indeed, Cecil Turtle is one of the few cartoon characters with the capacity to outwit the legendary Looney Tunes character Bugs Bunny, showing interesting interplay with the ancient theme of the trickster turtle. In 1941 Cecil Turtle featured in the short film 'Tortoise Beats Hare', an adaptation of the ancient story, written by Dave Monahan, for the popular cartoon series. Cecil's adversary in the race in the Looney Tunes version is Bugs Bunny. Interestingly, neither Cecil Turtle nor Bugs Bunny is referred to in the title of the short by his animal

'surname' of Turtle or Bunny, most likely to make the storyline of a competing hare and tortoise immediately recognizable.

The familiar story of the tortoise and the hare needs little introduction: the narrative has been described as 'the most well-known and enduring of Aesop's fables'.[2] The story is widely known but exists in many versions. Notable authors who have retold the story in verse include Jean de la Fontaine in 1668, and Marianne Moore in 1954.[3] In most accounts, the story unfolds with a boastful hare challenging a tortoise to a running race.

The tortoise accepts, and the two competitors commence their marathon. While the hare easily outpaces the tortoise, it decides to take a nap before the finish line, allowing the tortoise, with its steady pace, to overtake it, and win. The story's moral is that using speed and haste in an endeavour is not necessarily better than a slow and steady approach.

The story subtly compares the conscientiousness of the turtle, proceeding resolutely in awareness of his own shortcomings, with the arrogance and carelessness of the hare. Despite the overt narrative focus on speed, in the story of the tortoise and the hare, it is the attitudes of the two competitors, rather than their athletic capacities, which most emphatically decide the outcome of the contest. A tortoise and a hare are the most commonly depicted competing creatures in traditional stories, perhaps because this pairing fits the land setting of the race, and pits a notoriously quick animal (consider, for example, the expression 'haring

Western painted turtle takes a break from crossing a road at Sherburne National Wildlife Refuge in Minnesota.

Frans Snyders, *Fable of the Hare and the Tortoise*, between 1600 and 1657, oil on canvas.

around' for describing swift motion) against a creature famous for its lethargy. At times, however, there is some variety in the two contending animals, for example, in the Mayan folk tale of the turtle and the deer.

In the Looney Tunes versions, Bugs Bunny is outsmarted by the trickster turtle on three occasions. In the first race, featured in 'Tortoise Beats Hare' (1941), Cecil uses lookalike relatives to

Crane and Tortoise puppets, from the 2014 film of the same name directed by Matty Sidle.

keep pace with his speedy competitor, and wins the race by cheating. In 'Tortoise Wins by a Hare' (1943), Cecil wins through trickery once again, with the unwitting assistance of a group of mobsters who have laid bets on the race's outcome. Bugs Bunny finally wins a race against the tricky turtle in 'Rabbit Transit' (1947), but Cecil again outwits him, getting the rabbit arrested for speeding. Although much creative licence is taken with the folk story in the Looney Tunes versions, the cartoons retain the original narrative emphasis on the attitude of the competitors being more important than physical capacity for speed.

In the genre of children's entertainment, we move from cartoons to puppets – an area where, as in the cartoons above, the turtle's biology provides a basis for new artistic manifestations of the animal. These modern creations at times engage with the creature's ancient mythical roles.

A turtle puppet was used to engage with social issues on the children's educational series *Sesame Street*. From its original airing in 1969, *Sesame Street* has had a colourful cast of animal characters. Some of the animals, such as Big Bird, Bert and Ernie, and the Three Bears, are based on real animals (including humans), but many *Sesame Street* characters are based on fantastical creatures, such as monsters (for example, Grover, Elmo and the Cookie Monster), and even vampires (Count von Count, also known as 'The Count'). The presence of anthropomorphized animals is used on *Sesame Street* to create characters that are relatable to children, and the animals help to introduce children to new concepts and societal issues.

Sheldon 'Shelley' Turtle appears in numerous episodes of *Sesame Street*. Shelley's lack of flippers means that by some systems of classification, he would be considered a tortoise, but the character's epithet reflects the American tradition of referring to all chelonids as 'turtles'. The biological realities of the turtle inform the *Sesame Street* character. Shelley's home is a pond, he is slow-moving and he lives in his shell. The slowness associated with turtles is part of Shelley's characterization. Indeed, in one episode, he sings a song about how, despite the extra time it takes him to get anywhere, he does reach his planned destination in the end. The need for Shelley to progress through life at his own pace, and not allow himself to be rushed, is a message to which the series' young audience could likely relate. Although friendly, Shelley is shy. Shelley the Turtle's shyness relates to the traditional use of turtle imagery to explore social shyness in humans. Shy people are often said to be afraid to 'come out of their shells'. This analogy reflects the observation of turtles, when threatened, retreating into the safety of their shells.

In one *Sesame Street* episode, music teacher Bob Johnson (Bob McGrath) reads a story called 'The Turtle Who Wanted to Make Friends'. While reading the story, Bob advises Shelley (voiced by Jim Henson) on how he needs to 'come out of his shell' if he wants to make friends. For Shelley, this is not easy, as he comments that going into one's shell is 'what turtles do' – reflecting the natural human quality of shyness.

Another turtle puppet can be seen in the children's series *Noddy*, based on the creation of children's author Enid Blyton. Sherman the Tank Turtle was added with several other puppet animals to increase the appeal of the British show in North American markets. The connection between turtles and the military, seen in Sherman the Tank Turtle, shows the wide reach of the warrior turtle motif. This motif is creatively presented in a further puppet incarnation of the turtle from popular culture – this time from the television show *The Muppets*.

Although not a dedicated member of the Muppets, a turtle features memorably in an episode of the popular children's show. The scene, featuring a turtle and the character 'the Swedish Chef', shows the writers of *The Muppets* playing upon some common elements of the animal's reception in modern-day culture, these being the reputation of the turtle as a culinary delicacy, and its frequent portrayal as a warrior. 'Turtle Soup' takes place in the kitchen, where the Swedish Chef is filming his fictional cooking show. The Swedish Chef is known for his unintelligible speech and singing while cooking, as well as his use of unconventional implements in the kitchen, such as tennis rackets and shotguns. It has long been noted that, despite his name, the chef's accent bears no resemblance to Swedish. Henson based his character's voice on a taped impression of mock Swedish by the screenwriter Marshall Brickman, who worked on the screenplay of *The Muppets: Sex and Violence*.[4]

The 'Turtle Soup' sketch appeared in episode 405 of *The Muppet Show*, which originally aired in November 1979. The scene begins with the turtle puppet situated on the chopping board, alongside a tall pot of boiling water with some onions added into it. This is a realistic touch, as onions were a common ingredient in turtle soup, but by the episode's airing in 1979, turtle soup had already experienced a sharp decline in popularity.

As the Swedish Chef prepares to cook the live (puppet) turtle, he sings his trademark song, famously ending with 'Bort, bort, bort!' He seizes a machete and attempts to cut off the turtle's head. This action shows disturbingly authentic engagement with historical instructions for making turtle soup found in many antique cookbooks. The Muppet turtle, however, ducks its head into its shell. In a comedic manner, the turtle then shows the ability to move its body around its shell, continuously evading the Chef. Next, the cooking episode becomes an arms race, as the Chef pulls out an oversized shotgun. In his unintelligible language, he warns the turtle of his impending death. In response, the turtle's shell slowly turns around to reveal twin cannons poking out, with the shell now a gun turret. The Chef yelps in alarm, the turtle tank fires, and the Chef collapses. The turtle emerges, victorious and laughing, from a hatch on top of the shell. While initially the turtle puppet tries to avoid conflict, its shell provides it with a military pedigree stretching back to the ancient past, one which has continued into modern popular culture.

COMIC BOOK TURTLES

Comic books contain a great diversity of presentations of turtles: while the animals are often presented positively, they do not always use their powers for good. The turtle's natural slowness places the animal in ideological contrast with the comic hero The Flash. The turtle's unhurried pace has inspired the character of one of the 'Scarlet Speedster's' primary enemies: Turtle. Turtle first appeared in *All Flash* #21, published in December 1945. The typical slowness of his namesake animal features prominently in Turtle's characterization. Turtle uses his slowness strategically, both to unhurriedly form ingenious plans, and to create weapons related to slow speed. One of Turtle's favourite criminal pursuits is to attempt to rob banks. The tendency of The Flash's enemies to attempt to subvert social order, and to redistribute wealth (generally to themselves), has been noted as topical in the Cold War context of the Golden Age Flash.[5]

Turtle's lack of success in beating The Flash proved no obstacle to his character's succession. A later character from DC Comics, named 'Turtle Man', followed the lead of the original Turtle in taking the slow and steady approach to supervillainy. As well as moving and plotting criminal escapades at a slow pace, Turtle Man used a shell of body armour to defend himself from zealous superheroes intent on thwarting his plans. Turtle Man was the first adversary faced by the new Flash, Barry Allen, in *Showcase 1* #4 (1956). The two slow-moving antagonists eventually team up – although at times it would seem that two turtles are one too many, with Turtle and Turtle Man facing some conflict with one another in *Flash 2* #35 (1990).

The character of Turtle also appears in the television series *The Flash*. In the Season 2 episode 'Potential Energy' (2016), the Flash (Grant Gustin) must battle against the Turtle (Aaron Douglas) in order to protect a loved one. Turtle in the television series employs a similar power his character has at times used in comic books: the ability to sap the speed of other people. The Flash is able to subdue Turtle, who is imprisoned and then murdered by the (occasionally) evil scientist Harrison Wells (Tom Cavanagh).

Another turtle-like creature who literally looms large in comic culture is Gamera. A giant monster who possesses the ability to fly, Gamera is further distinct among his fellow chelids for his ability to breath fire. Unlike the turtle-based characters from the Flash, Gamera is shown to have positive and protective qualities to his characterization, alongside the destructive and dangerous ones. Gamera is known as the 'friend to all children', and most of the storylines featured in his films involve the giant turtle befriending and protecting one or more young humans.

Gamera first appeared in Japanese *kaiju* films in the mid-1960s and early 1970s. *Kaiju* films are known for featuring giant monsters, who typically attack cities and frequently tangle with the military. Gamera, whose name means 'monster turtle', had his first appearance in the film *Gamera the Giant Monster* (1965). Gamera was initially conceived as a competitor for the huge success of Godzilla, arguably the most famous of Japanese *kaiju* films. The historical context of the Cold War is referenced in the original *Gamera* film from 1965, in which the prehistoric turtle is awakened by an atomic blast. The nuclear explosion is caused by the crash of a Soviet bomber following a skirmish with American fighter planes over the Arctic. The blast is sufficiently powerful to release Gamera from suspended animation in a large block of ice – an origin story which takes on added interest in the modern day, with the continuing ecological problem of melting polar icecaps.

Indeed, Gamera has been considered in academic works for its timely environmental themes. As noted by the opening scene of Gamera's nuclear awakening in the Arctic foregrounds, there is a focus on ecological concerns by juxtaposing 'the destructiveness and violence of human-made weaponry with the tranquil serenity

Gamera vs
Godzilla toys.

of the natural world'.[6] The use of environmental themes is a common element in the representation of turtles in popular culture, and a frequent motif in Japanese monster movies.

Many monster movies from various cultures provide a larger-than-life exploration of the relationship between humans and the natural world, and present the often-destructive consequences that follow from ecological imbalance. Numerous Western monster films present thematic concerns involving environmental destruction, where humanity's own damaging potential is contrasted against the dangerous power of the featured 'creature'. These concerns are shown in the characterization of Gamera, whose awakening through human violence creates environmental discord.

TEENAGE MUTANT NINJA TURTLES

Echoes of the turtle's ancient cultural symbolism are found in its appearance in popular culture in combat roles. The concept of turtle warriors underpins the Teenage Mutant Ninja Turtles (henceforth TMNT), characters found in comics, video games, television series, films and more. While 'turtle power' is not a modern phenomenon, the characterization of the TMNT as young and cool sees them playing against traditional turtle type.

The TMNT are a four-strong group of comic book heroes in a half-shell who have moulded and dominated the popular image of the turtle in the modern day. As well as being imagined as warriors for millennia, turtles have long held a reputation for secrecy. The hidden quality of the turtle, tucked up in its shell, creates a mysterious image that is a good fit for the 'ninja' aspect of the cartoon heroes.

The ancient connection between turtles and martial expertise has been cleverly modernized in the image of the TMNT. The

'teenage' part of the turtle squad has translated into four heroes who are seamlessly aligned with the modern teenage culture of the time of their creation – the 1980s and '90s.

The turtles love fast food – notably pizza – watch television and listen to contemporary music. The four of them speak in a distinctive vernacular associated with the Californian surfing community – Michelangelo's catchphrase of 'Cowabunga, dude!' was coined in the first episode of the cartoon series, as he surfed atop a filing cabinet in a flooded building. While warrior turtles are ancient, and turtles themselves prehistoric, the TMNT are coolly fashionable and recognizably at home in their modern cultural context. Adding to the temporal mix is the comic writers' choice to name each of the Turtles after a famous painter of the Renaissance period: Donatello, Leonardo, Raphael and Michelangelo.

'Turtle power' is a key element of the team's success, but the influence of the TMNT has had a broad and perhaps unexpected

The four heroes of *Teenage Mutant Ninja Turtles II – The Secret of the Ooze* (1991).

result beyond the purchase of comic books and action figures. The popularity of the TMNT has had a powerful effect on the science of herpetology, and on the conservation movement. A phenomenon observed by many in the field of herpetology is the positive role of the TMNT in awakening greater interest in the study and conservation of turtles. In an example of life reflecting art, the heroes in the half-shell continue to have a significant impact on the fortunes of their reptile-like relatives in the natural world.

The TMNT first appeared in a comic created by Kevin Eastman and Peter Laird in 1984 (*Teenage Mutant Ninja Turtles* #1). The early comic shows the four combatants fighting against their arch-nemesis, the evil Shredder, and his army, the Foot (a homage to fellow superhero Daredevil's enemy, the Hand). The early comics featuring the TMNT are edgier in tone than the syndicated cartoon show of the same name that launched in 1986, which ran until 1996.

While there are moments of humour and camaraderie between the comic turtles, their individual personalities and 'teenage' qualities are given greater focus in the television series. Emphasizing the distinctiveness of each turtle's personality was a conscious decision to help the audience to bond with the half-shelled heroes. Each turtle's characterization enhanced aspects of their comic book identities, while also working to appeal to the new audience of television viewers.[7] The changes included introducing the TMNT's famous love of pizza (which is not recommended for non-mutant turtles).

The TMNT leverage their animal attributes to make them more powerful warriors. The Turtles frequently use their shells as armour. In the 2014 film *Teenage Mutant Ninja Turtles*, the warriors use their hard shells to protect themselves and their reporter friend, April O'Neil (Megan Fox), from gunfire. At other times, the four heroes show the handy ability of some turtles to retract their heads into their shells. This ability is a key component of the 'Head Droppin'' variety of TMNT action figures, which developed in the 1990s.

The TMNT have appeared in countless incarnations and continue to find new audiences. In 2018 a new cartoon series was launched: *Rise of the Teenage Mutant Ninja Turtles*. In this series, each warrior is imagined as a different species of turtle. Raphael is a snapping turtle, Leonardo a red-eared slider, Michelangelo a box-shell turtle and Donatello a soft-shell turtle, who at times wears a 'battle shell'. The separate species show the creators' continued interest in allowing the warrior-turtles to be easily distinguishable from one another, but also demonstrates that their 'turtle power' remains at the heart of their image.

Moving to the other end of the age spectrum in terms of turtle protagonists, in the film *Kung Fu Panda* (2008) an ancient turtle martial-arts master named Oogway gives Zen-like guidance to his young panda protégé, Po. The character of Oogway (voiced by Randall Duk Kim) connects the wisdom associated with turtles with their frequent identification as warriors. Oogway's characterization adheres to traditional turtle tropes, giving Po's uniqueness as a rotund panda warrior increased emphasis. Despite his age, Oogway is considered the only character among the animals to be capable of defeating the villainous snow leopard Tai Lung (Ian McShane).

The connection of turtles with wisdom is given a fresh perspective in the 2003 animated film *Finding Nemo*. The film follows the journey of a clownfish protagonist named Marlin as he searches for his missing son, Nemo. The anxieties of parenthood and questions of how to deal with life's uncertainties are thematically explored in the film, with Marlin receiving help and some sage advice from a turtle named Crush. The turtles in the film rescue

Marlin and his regal blue tang fish companion, Dory, and help them to reach Sydney Harbour. Crush has been referred to as a 'surfer turtle', due to his laid-back speech, use of surfing vernacular, 'waxing' of his shell and relaxed athleticism when riding the East Australian Current. The long association with surfing and mindfulness is present in Crush's advice to Marlin that he let his parenting be guided by his offspring's cues, and his admission that when it comes to timing, 'you never really know'. The scene of Crush's parenting advice shows creative interplay with the reality of turtle parenting, with the hatchlings needing to find their own way back to the ocean following birth.

There is a shadow side to the use of cartoon turtles to connect with young audiences. Bert the Turtle is the star of *Duck and Cover*, a series of instructional films issued by the U.S. Federal Civil Defense Administration in the 1950s. The films were a response from the government to the threat of nuclear war, and were shown to schoolchildren to teach them how to react in the event of a nuclear attack. The use of a cartoon turtle in the short civic defence films helped to communicate frightening information about nuclear strikes in an accessible way, and to an extent diminish the threat in the minds of the child audience.[8] Bert is a

Master Oogway shares his wisdom in *Kung Fu Panda*.

debonair-looking turtle with a hat and bow tie, and he is described as clever and careful. Children were urged to follow Bert's example, and to dive for cover in the event of a nuclear strike.

For Bert, finding cover was shown to be as simple as folding up inside his shell, with the children instead having to find desks or chairs. As well as carrying his nuclear shield on his back, Bert's use as *Duck and Cover*'s mascot capitalizes on the sympathy of children for turtle animals, and turtles' reputation as friendly creatures. Of course, turtle shells are not radiation-proof (or bulletproof, except in the case of turtles of the TMNT variety).

Despite this factual oversight, Bert's campaign to 'duck and cover' had surprisingly long-lasting influence. Bert has been connected to the increased construction of fallout shelters in the United States during the Cold War, when many Americans grew 'shells – like the turtle's – affixed to their collective backs'.[9] The need to 'duck and cover' influenced the architecture of school buildings and community centres under the Kennedy administration, transforming the 'shape and materials of American suburban architecture to economically and unobtrusively offer maximum protection'.[10]

The appearance of turtles in popular culture has had a significant impact on their perception in contemporary human thought. The TMNT have provided turtle public relations with an enormous boost, and the large numbers of cartoon and puppet turtle characters generally, but not exclusively, emphasize the animal's positive and popular image. The turtle's shell looms large in modern popular culture. While the shell is a ubiquitous part of the pop culture turtle, its use shows great diversification – it may offer protection, provide a place to store ammunition or even present an obstacle to social engagement. The variety in the use of the turtle's shell demonstrates the capacity of the chelid's distinctive anatomy to fuel the human imagination. The appearance of turtles in popular culture is shaped, but by no means defined, by their natural qualities.

In children's entertainment, the slow, shy reputation of the turtle makes it a popular protagonist, relatable for young audiences. These audiences may then identify with the 'underdog' turtles who subvert the limitations of their physical forms to become powerful figures, and sometimes, even heroes (in a half-shell).

7 The Turtle's Tail: The Environment and the Future

The turtle never abandons its carriage.
Lesotho proverb

Turtles have survived and thrived for many millions of years, colonizing every continent except Antarctica, and inhabiting every ocean but the Arctic and Antarctic. In more recent times, a combination of human-led factors have created a conservational crisis for the turtle, resulting in all seven species of sea turtle now being endangered or threatened. Yet the turtle's reputation in ancient myths for persistence and hardiness is in many ways reflective of the biological animal. As it weathers the environmental storm, the turtle is proving a powerful ally in human efforts to preserve earth's ecological riches. Turtle-based ecotourism has provided economic incentives for the protection of delicate ecosystems, and the animal's enduring popularity makes it a compelling ambassador for the issue of habitat preservation. Often considered a modern phenomenon, the turtle's connection to conservation can be traced back almost five hundred years. The modern-day identification of the turtle as a kind of eco-warrior among animals draws upon its ancient cultural symbolism and the animal's graceful charisma and popularity.

In 2017 there were 356 turtle species recognized worldwide. These turtles were catalogued through the efforts of the Turtle Taxonomy Group, an informal working group of the Tortoise and Freshwater Turtle Specialist Group, a team of experts who have collected data on living and newly extinct turtles since 2007. Of these known turtle species, approximately 61 per cent are either currently threatened, or already extinct. This precipitous decline in turtle biodiversity is a result of many factors, notably habitat destruction, unsustainable overexploitation and climate change.[1] It is clear, then, that the increasingly significant global issue of conservation is very much an area of interest for the turtle.

Recent studies have shown that turtles are useful as bioindicators, with their success or otherwise giving a good indication of the health of their environment overall. Turtles are also crucially important in preserving the health of their own habitats. Turtles who burrow provide shelter for many creatures, and in their movements across different terrains, turtles are important dispersers of seeds.

The environmental issue of light pollution has been shown in recent studies to be of vital significance to both humans and turtles. Artificial light at night-time can cause the normal rhythms and routines of animals, including reptiles, birds, turtles and humans, to be inhibited. Artificial lighting interferes with visual clues needed by nesting turtles to find optimal nesting sites. The problem of light pollution is perhaps most keenly felt by hatchlings, who rely on light to direct them safely to the sea. For millions of years, the reflected light from the Moon and stars sparkling on the ocean's surface has proved a guide for baby turtles. In the modern day, the hatchlings' attraction to light has become a road to disaster rather than a path to salvation, with the baby turtles unknowingly turning from the ocean and heading towards busy roads and other brightly lit areas. Many charitable foundations and volunteers now work to try to shield the baby turtles from the problem of artificial lighting, as well as predation by feral or introduced animals, and poaching.

The awareness of the threat posed to hatchlings by artificial light has been accompanied by an increasing concern in scientific

Turtle-safe lamps light the Tarague Beach recreational area, 17 August 2014, on Andersen Air Force Base, Guam.

communities about the dangers posed to turtles by climate change. Turtle eggs have been found to depend on their surrounding temperatures for gender selection. If the sand surrounding the eggs is warmer, more hatchlings will be female compared to cooler nests (usually less than 29°c). With increasing temperatures, conservationists have become concerned that the natural balance of male and female turtle hatchlings (which historically tended to slightly favour the female turtles) may be in danger. A lack of male turtles could have significant effects on the numbers of turtle populations, as a male turtle may mate with numerous females in a breeding setting. Turtle eggs can only incubate within a narrow range of temperatures, meaning that extreme temperature fluctuations may result not in a greater gender imbalance among turtle hatchlings, but in no hatchlings at all. Researchers and volunteers are trialling new methods to keep turtle nests at a viable temperature, through the use of shading, and at times, nest relocation.

In recent years, turtles have come to play an important role in the international ecotourism business. Ecotourism has been defined as travel with a primary interest in the natural history of a destination.[2] Turtles may be involved in ecotourism in a number of ways (for example, they can be a featured animal in a zoo or an aquarium). Ecotourists may journey to spot turtles in their natural habitats, or to take a more active role in rescuing and preserving wild turtles. Perhaps the best-known activities for tourists involving turtles relate to the animals' nesting and hatching behaviours. The seasonal appearance of pregnant turtles on often-remote beaches in recent years has been accompanied by the arrival of tourists, wishing to experience at first hand the remarkable nesting and egg-laying behaviours of turtles. Once the eggs reach maturity, their hatching provides a second opportunity to see baby turtles take part in the first steps of their life journey, as the hatchlings make their way from land to water.

The developing area of ecotourism is a field with great potential to promote the interests of both humans and turtles. Communities may benefit financially from the capacity of turtles to draw visitors to often remote places, and the animals themselves benefit from increased awareness among touring turtle enthusiasts of current conservation issues. The longer history of turtle tourism, however,

A Kemp's Ridley sea turtle gets a ride home from the U.S. Coast Guard.

Loggerhead turtle hatchling on the sand at a u.s. National Wildlife Refuge on Roanoke Island, North Carolina.

provides numerous examples of ways in which tourists and turtles should not be paired. Perhaps the best-known example of historical turtle tourism is the promotion of the 'sport' of turtle riding on Australia's Great Barrier Reef in the early twentieth century. Turtle riding reached peak popularity in the 1920s and '30s. During nesting season, tourists would waylay female turtles, as the creatures attempted to return to the water after laying eggs. If the turtle riding was to occur later in the day, the turtles would be tipped upside down to wait until the agreed time. Once a party of turtle riders had assembled, the participant would climb onto the turtle's back, holding themselves in place by gripping the edges of the shell. Doubtlessly exhausted from nesting, labouring and attempting to avoid vacuous vacationers, the turtle would nonetheless attempt to return to the ocean, with the human riding on their back. Once in the water, the turtle would most often swiftly escape into the depths.

By the 1960s turtle riding had all but disappeared, and was no longer used to promote tourism to the Reef.[3] The disappearance of turtle riding is not thought to be connected to apprehensions around the animal's welfare, but to the development of new, less-invasive ways for tourists to interact with the Reef, such as the construction of underwater viewing stations and the rise of scuba

diving.[4] This is in contrast to the concerned response to the growth of the Reef's turtle canneries, operating around the same historical period.

TURTLES AS PETS AND THE ILLEGAL WILDLIFE TRADE

Moving from ecotravel to more domestic matters, the universal appeal of turtles as pets has seen various species embraced as part of the household, from Belize to Tanzania. The popularity of the pet turtle increased exponentially during the 1950s, and this surge in demand fuelled the proliferation of turtle farms in the southern United States.[5] These farms shipped turtles (typically red-eared slider hatchlings) to fulfil the demands of the domestic and international market – during this time, the United States was the largest supplier of turtles to the international pet trade.[6] The pet turtle is considered good company and may be long-lived – although the animal's longevity might not be sufficient for all pet-owners. When offered a pet turtle as a gift, Fidel Castro – himself renowned for his unusual durability – declined the animal, after hearing it would likely live for 'only' one hundred years. 'That's the problem with pets,' Castro said. 'You get attached to them and then they die on you.'[7]

The popularity of turtles in the pet trade presents something of a mixed blessing for the animal. On the one hand, the appreciation and affection that turtle-owners have for their pets contributes to public awareness of different breeds of turtle, their habitats and behaviours, and welfare. On the other hand, keeping turtles as pets may be hazardous for both the owner and the animal. First, we explore the dangers posed to the turtle by the illegal exotic pet trade, and then consider whether turtles may be hazardous to human health.

The illegal trade of wildlife is a multibillion-dollar industry, often run by criminal syndicates, operating in remote regions and exploiting local people.[8] The trade in illegal wildlife is now worth at least $19 billion annually, meaning that it sits alongside drug trafficking, arms smuggling and the trafficking of human slaves in terms of illicit profit.[9] Along with the trafficking of humans, animal trafficking has been identified as one of the fastest-growing illegal markets, and frequently the networks used by cartels for illegal wildlife trading are also utilized for other illicit trade, such as weapons or drugs.[10]

The growth of the illegal wildlife trade in the past ten years has been significant. This increase has been fuelled by an upsurge in affluence in regions where animals are sought for their use in traditional medicines, food or, for many species, their appeal as novelty pets. At the same time, penalties for the illegal trade of animals are frequently lighter than those for trafficking in the comparably sized markets of drugs, arms and humans, further fuelling the growth of the illicit industry. Reptiles comprise an estimated 21 per cent of the value of the live animal trade, with turtles being counted as one of the more popular types of trafficked 'reptile'.[11]

The enormous amounts of money at stake and the involvement of major criminal networks make attempts to stop wildlife trading inherently dangerous.[12] Trafficking in turtle eggs is seen as a lucrative sideline for drug cartels.[13] The risks involved in protecting turtles from wildlife trafficking were recently highlighted by the tragic death of Jairo Mora Sandoval. A Costa Rican environmentalist, Mora Sandoval was kidnapped and murdered by a group of men poaching turtle eggs in 2013. Tensions around turtle poaching in the area had been escalating for some time. In 2012 men armed with AK-47s raided a hatchery for baby turtles.[14] In the weeks prior to Mora Sandoval's death, he had reached out to friends on social media to try to mobilize local authorities to stop egg thieves preying on nesting sea turtles at Moin beach in Costa Rica.[15]

Mora Sandoval's death created an international outcry, including a formal statement from the United Nations. The

Turtle eggs for sale at Kota Bharu market in Malaysia.

Environmentalist Jairo Mora Sandoval working at the turtle egg hatchery of the Ostional beach Leatherback and Pacific Green Sea Turtle Project with fellow volunteers in 2011.

young conservationist's murder highlights the pressing need for international authorities to recognize and respond to the dangers posed by the illegal wildlife trade. Mora Sandoval's story also demonstrates the remarkable courage and dedication displayed by many working in the field of conservation.

Even those who work within law enforcement are not immune to the threats posed by poachers. In July 2018 a patrol car belonging to the Royal Cayman Islands Police Service was involved in a crash with a vehicle driven by turtle smugglers. The police were responding to a call about a turtle in distress. A staff member from the Cayman Turtle Centre (CTC) raised the alarm about the presence of the smugglers, with some reports suggesting the poachers had threatened CTC staff with a knife.[16] Despite the involvement of police and media attention, poachers were again hunting turtles on the beaches of the Cayman Islands a few nights later – although in this instance, the involvement of the public meant the turtle

in question could be saved. The turtle went on to nest and lay her
eggs the following evening.[17]

The danger to the global environment presented by wildlife
trafficking is twofold, involving a loss of biodiversity and the
transmission of zoonotic (transferred between species) and other
diseases.[18] As well as having catastrophic cultural and environmental consequences, the loss in biodiversity is considered to
have serious economic consequences. A recent report stated that
in Africa, the illegal poaching of elephants alone cost around £4
billion in lost natural capital.[19] The transmission of diseases
through trafficking in exotic animals can cause human outbreaks,
as well as threatening livestock, international trade, rural liveli-
hoods, native wildlife populations and the health of ecosystems.[20]
A disease with numerous widely reported outbreaks related to
illegal turtle trafficking is salmonellosis.[21]

In recent years, it has become increasingly common knowledge that turtles require careful handling, and present health and

safety risks to their owners. Due to the enduring appeal of turtles for children, these health risks are especially worthy of note. Health risks from turtles played a central role in the decline of turtle farming for the international pet trade in the United States. In May 1975 the American Food and Drug Administration (FDA) banned the sale of pet turtles, citing thousands of cases of severe illness in humans.[22] At one stage, the FDA estimated that turtles were responsible for over a quarter of a million cases of salmonellosis in the United States annually. A statement from the FDA commissioner, Alexander M. Schmidt, cited the risk of pathogenic organisms being transmitted from turtles to humans. The *New York Times* noted the particular risk of transmission from turtles of salmonella bacteria, which the article observed may be 'easily transmitted to children if they handle the pets and then touch their mouth or food without washing'.[23] Turtles often carry salmonella bacteria on their skins and shells. While harmless to the animal, if transmitted to humans the bacteria can result in serious health problems. Despite the 1975 ban, turtles continue to be linked to numerous multi-state outbreaks of salmonellosis in the United States.

In recent years, turtles have experienced a renewed upsurge of popularity as pets. Their appeal is reflected in numerous pet turtles playing minor roles in popular television shows and film, where the animals are often associated with characters who may appear somewhat eccentric. In the film *Beverly Hills Cop II* (1987), Officer Billy Rosewood (Judge Reinhold) has a turtle named Big Al, who fits well into the character's unusually verdant home. Big Al is the target of teasing from the series' hero, Axel Foley (Eddie Murphy), who notes the practical difficulties involved in turtle sexing and mating. Sherlock Holmes (Jonny Lee Miller) has a pet turtle named Clyde in the series *Elementary*, with the animal proving to be a fan favourite. Fans of the show *Stranger Things* showed a similar affection for the pet of Dustin (Gaten Matarazzo), a turtle named Yertle.

The increasing visibility of turtles in popular culture has led to a greater interest in their value as pets. With this interest has come a rise in the incidence of salmonellosis from turtle-handling in the u.s.[24] While the ban on selling small turtles remains in place, some traders have attempted to circumnavigate it with strategies such as giving away turtle hatchlings to customers who buy turtle enclosures. Other turtle pets may have been rescued and adopted by their human companions, in an attempt to give the animals a better life.

TURTLE COUP?

The last word on turtles in this book goes to a turtle in Uganda. In the late 1970s, the East African country saw a regime change involving not just politicians talking about turtles, but turtles talking about politics. The military dictatorship of Idi Amin Dada Oumee (better known as Idi Amin) came to an end in the late 1970s. Presaging this regime change was a creature from African folklore – a talking turtle.

In an intriguing blend of politics and popular culture, rumours of a talking turtle spread through Uganda a few weeks before Uganda's Independence Day (9 October) in 1978. As reported in *Jet* magazine, the turtle was said to be travelling around near the capital Kampala, spreading 'rumours' about Amin's government.[25] A talking tortoise known as Enfudu is associated with the Baganda culture of East Africa.

The activities of the talking turtle were reported on Radio Kampala. The animal was said to have slowly made its way to a police station. Once there, it prophesied the fall of Amin's government, and requested an audience with the governor and the

Tab.XXVIII.

1. Test. denticulata L.z.3.Test. signata Walb.

Illustration of a speckled tortoise (*Testudo signata*, now called *Chersobius signatus*) from Johann David Schöpf, *Historia testudinum iconibus illustrata* (1792).

police commissioner. Amin was said to be so disturbed by stories of the appearance of the folkloric creature that he gave the order that anyone who was found to propagate stories about the turtle would be executed by firing squad. Despite Amin's efforts, the giant turtle continued to evade capture for some time, before the government finally reported they had arrested the animal. Locking up the loquacious chelid would not solve the problems in Amin's government, however, and the regime fell in 1979.

At the end of this survey, there is much about the turtle that remains enigmatic. The cultural symbolism of turtles from a variety of historical and geographic settings presents the animal as a remarkable example of balance for its capacity to inhabit and embody numerous extremes. By turns physically hard and soft, and able to survive on land and in water, the turtle's biological dichotomy is reflected in its cultural image. Through many millennia of human thought, the turtle has been connected to the creation and protection of the earth, yet it also has a mythological role as a hardened warrior, capable of causing damage and destruction.

Turtles are among the most threatened groups of animals in the world. A landmark 2018 study showed that turtles were more threatened than birds, fish, mammals and even the 'much besieged' amphibians.[26] Turtles are connected with 'home' in human thought, particularly through the biological myth of the turtle 'carrying its home on its back'. The relationship between turtle and shell is mirrored in the relationship between all living things and the environment. Like the turtle, none of the world's living inhabitants can leave the protective 'shell' of the earth's biosphere (human, turtle and other animal astronauts excepted). The increasing awareness of the need to protect turtles and their environment gives some cause for optimism. Greater scientific monitoring and new technologies mean the near future will yield exciting new knowledge about turtles. New species of turtle are still being found, and an example of this trend may be seen in the discovery in 2018 of a new species of mud turtle in western Mexico, *Kinosternon vogti*.

In the story of the tortoise and the hare, it is the attitude of the two contestants, rather than their physical capabilities, which decides the race. Studying the image of the turtle throughout human history allows a pause to appreciate the graceful qualities of the creature's physiology, and its remarkable evolutionary persistence. A notably slow animal, showing little aggression, the turtle has a complicated life cycle that involves conquering significant obstacles. With the odds of survival seemingly stacked against it, there is something magical, and even hopeful, about the endurance of the turtle.

Timeline of the Turtle

240 MYA	230 MYA	210 MYA	1500–900 BCE
Extinct turtle *Pappochelys rosinae* lives alongside the first known species of dinosaur	An ancient turtle named *Eorhynchochelys sinensis* has a beak, but no shell	*Proganochelys quenstedti*, a toothed turtle, lives in the Late Triassic	Turtles appear in the pre-Columbian Mayan record, the Madrid Codex

17th century CE	1620 CE	1711
Turtles commonly appear in netsuke, distinctive miniature sculptures created in Japan, originally to address the absence of pockets in kimonos	The island of Bermuda passes an Act to protect turtles from slaughter in response to declining populations, marking a significant milestone in the development of environmental conservation	Jamaica passes a law protecting turtle eggs from poachers

1952	1957	1968	1984
Archie Carr publishes *Handbook for Turtles*	Dr Seuss's classic *Yertle the Turtle and Other Stories* is published	The Soviet spacecraft *Zond 5* is fired into orbit, carrying turtle cosmonauts	Kevin Eastman and Peter Laird create the half-shelled heroes the Teenage Mutant Ninja Turtles, in their first comic

Mid-second millennium BCE–228 BCE	11th century BCE	550 BCE

Turtles feature in the *Šumma Alu* omens from ancient Mesopotamia

An elderly shaman woman is buried with more than fifty turtles in Canaan

Greek silver *stater* coins produced on the island of Aegina, bearing a turtle on one side

1883	1908	1930	1950s

Jonathan, a Seychelles giant tortoise (*Aldabrachelys gigantea hololissa*), is born. Considered to be the world's oldest living turtle

Henri Matisse paints *Bathers with a Turtle*

Al Capone makes an ill-fated move into turtle racing

The U.S. government uses Bert the Turtle to teach schoolchildren how to respond to nuclear threats in the *Duck and Cover* instructional videos

2004	2013	2015

Timmy the Turtle, the last living participant in the Crimean War, dies at 160 years of age

Aosta Rican environmentalist Jairo Mora Sandoval is kidnapped and murdered while protecting turtle nests

A species of turtle in the South Pacific is found to be the first biofluorescent 'reptile' ever found in the wild

References

INTRODUCTION: SWIMMING IN THE SLOW LANE WITH TURTLES

1 Blair E. Witherington, *Sea Turtles: An Extraordinary Natural History of Some Uncommon Turtles* (St Paul, MN, 2006), p. 15.
2 E. G. Wilson et al., 'Why Healthy Oceans Need Sea Turtles: The Importance of Sea Turtles to Marine Ecosystems', https://oceana.org, accessed 24 November 2018.
3 C. H. Ernst and J. E. Lovich, *Turtles of the United States and Canada*, 2nd edn (Baltimore, MD, 2009), p. 3.

1 A BASIC GUIDE TO TURTLE ZOOLOGY

1 Peter L. Lutz and John A. Musick, eds, *The Biology of Sea Turtles* (Boca Raton, FL, 1997), pp. 1–2.
2 Kate Maccord et al., 'The Dawn of Chelonian Research: Turtles between Comparative Anatomy and Embryology in the 19th Century', *Journal of Experimental Zoology Part B: Molecular and Developmental Evolution*, CCCXXIV/3 (2015), pp. 169–80.
3 Ibid., p. 179.
4 James H. Harding, 'What, If Anything, Is a Reptile?' *Bulletin of the Chicago Herpetological Society*, XL/8 (2006), pp. 141–6.
5 T. R. Lyson et al., 'Fossorial Origin of the Turtle Shell', *Current Biology*, XXVI/14 (2016), pp. 1887–94.
6 Ibid.

7   Jeanette Wyneken, 'Sea Turtle Locomotion: Mechanisms,
    Behavior, and Energetics', in *The Biology of Sea Turtles*,
    ed. Peter L. Lutz and John A. Musik (Boca Raton, FL, 1997),
    p. 193.
8   J. A. Fujii et al., 'Limb-use by Foraging Marine Turtles, an
    Evolutionary Perspective', PeerJ 6:e4565, www.ncbi.nlm.nih.gov,
    28 March 2018.
9   Joe Pinkstone, 'Sea Turtles Use Their Flippers Like HANDS to
    Karate-chop Jellyfish, Play with Their Food and Lick Their
    "Fingers" After Eating', www.dailymail.co.uk, 28 March 2018.
10 Maurice Burton and Robert Burton, *Marshall Cavendish
    International Wildlife Encyclopedia* (Singapore, 1994), p. 2300.
11 Ronald Orenstein, *Turtles, Tortoises and Terrapins: Survivors in
    Armor* (Buffalo, NY, 2001), p. 174.
12 Paul Rose, 'Never, Ever Interrupt Mating Giant Tortoises',
    blog.nationalgeographic.org, 17 March 2015.
13 S. Milton, 'Insights into Aging from Turtles, Animals that Show
    Extremely Slow Aging', *The Gerontologist* LX/2 (2015), p. 383.
14 J. W. Gibbons, 'Aging Phenomena in Reptiles', in *Special Review
    of Experimental Aging Research*, ed. M. F. Elias, B. E. Eleftheriou
    and P. K. Elias (Bar Harbor, ME, 1976), pp. 454–75.
15 Graeme Hays, 'Space Tracking Reveals Turtles' Record-breaking
    Ocean Swim', theconversation.com, 22 July 2014.
16 Ibid.
17 V. A. Stiebens et al., 'Living on the Edge: How Philopatry
    Maintains Adaptive Potential', *Proceedings of the Royal Society B:
    Biological Sciences*, CCLXXX (2013), p. 1763.
18 J. Roger Brothers and Kenneth J. Lohmann, 'Evidence that
    Magnetic Navigation and Geomagnetic Imprinting Shape Spatial
    Genetic Variation in Sea Turtles', *Current Biology*, XXVIII/8 (2018),
    pp. 1325–9.
19 Milagros López-Mendilaharsu et al., 'Prolonged Deep Dives by
    the Leatherback Turtle *Dermochelys coriacea*: Pushing Their Aerobic
    Dive Limits', *Marine Biodiversity Records*, II (2009), pp. 1–4.
20 Carl J. Franklin, *Turtles: An Extraordinary Natural History 245
    Million Years in the Making* (St Paul, MN, 2007), p. 13.

21 Orenstein, *Turtles*, p. 2.

22 Ibid.

23 James R. Spotila, *Sea Turtles: A Complete Guide to Their Biology, Behavior, and Conservation* (Baltimore, MD, 2004), p. 46.

24 Francesca Soldati et al., 'Long-term Memory of Relative Reward Values', *Biology Letters*, XIII/2, rsbl.royalsocietypublishing.org, 1 February 2017.

25 Camila Rudge Ferrara et al., 'Sound Communication and Social Behavior in an Amazonian River Turtle (*Podocnemis expansa*)', *Herpetologica*, LXX/2 (2014), pp. 149–56.

26 Camila Ferrara et al., 'Chelonian Vocal Communication', in *Biocommunication of Animals*, ed. Guenther Witzany (Dordrecht, 2014), pp. 261–74.

27 Vincenzo Ferri, *Tortoises and Turtles* (Willowdale, ON, 2002), p. 11.

2 TURTLES IN THE ANCIENT WORLD

1 Remi Berthon et al., 'Buried with Turtles: The Symbolic Role of the Euphrates Soft-shelled Turtle (*Rafetus euphraticus*) in Mesopotamia', *Antiquity*, XC/349 (2016), pp. 111–25.

2 Ibid.

3 Karen Rhea Nemet-Nejat, *Daily Life in Ancient Mesopotamia* (Westport, CT, 1998), p. 81.

4 Berthon et al., 'Buried with Turtles', pp. 111–25.

5 Sally M. Freedman, *If a City Is Set on a Height: The Akkadian Omen Series Shumma Alu ina Mele . . . Shumma Alu*, vol. III *(Tablets 41–63)* (Winona Lake, IN, 2017), p. 156.

6 Ibid., p. 156.

7 J. A. Black et al., eds, 'Gilgamesh, Enki, and the Netherworld', lines 47–69, www.etcsl.orient.ox.ac.uk, accessed 5 October 2018.

8 Jeremy Black and Anthony Green, eds, *Gods, Demons and Symbols of Mesopotamia* (London, 1992), p. 179.

9 Tallay Ornan, *The Triumph of the Symbol: Pictorial Representation of Deities in Mesopotamia and the Biblical Image Ban* (Göttingen, 2005), p. 130.

10   J. A. Black et al., eds, 'The Heron and the Turtle', lines 60–66, etcsl.orinst.ox.ac.uk, accessed 1 June 2018.

11   Julian Pas and Man Kam Leung, *Historical Dictionary of Taoism* (Lanham, MD, 1998), p. 52.

12   Sian Lewis and Lloyd Llewellyn-Jones, *The Culture of Animals in Antiquity: A Sourcebook with Commentaries* (London, 2018).

13   Eleanor Harris, *Ancient Egyptian Magic* (Newburyport, MA, 2016), p. 49.

14   Berthon et al., 'Buried with Turtles', pp. 111–25.

15   Ibid.

16   Kenneth R. Weiss, 'Pope Asked to Call Sea Turtles "Meat"', *Los Angeles Times* (14 March 2002), www.latimes.com/archives; 'Pope Asked to Label Turtles Meat, Not Fish', *Chicago Tribune* (15 March 2002), www.chicagotribune.com, accessed 11 December 2019.

17   Kenneth Sheedy, 'Aegina, the Cyclades, and Crete', in *The Oxford Handbook of Greek and Roman Coinage*, ed. William E. Metcalf, www.oxfordhandbooks.com, November 2012, pp. 106–7.

18   Sarah B. Pomeroy, *Women in Hellenistic Egypt: From Alexander to Cleopatra* (Detroit, MI, 1990), p. 33.

19   John James Audubon, Lucy Green Bakewell Audubon and Robert Williams Buchanan, *The Life and Adventures of John James Audubon, the Naturalist* (London, 1868).

20   Pomeroy, *Women*, p. 34.

21   Alastair Harden, *Animals in the Classical World: Ethical Perspectives from Greek and Roman Texts* (Basingstoke, 2013).

22   Pausanius, *Description of Greece*, 1.44.8 (Cambridge, MA, 1918).

23   Jocelyn M. C. Toynbee, *Animals in Roman Life and Art* (Ithaca, NY, 1973), p. 222.

24   Ibid.

25   John James Collins, *Native American Religions: A Geographical Survey* (Lewiston, NY, 1991), p. 309.

26   Gerardo Reichel Dolmatoff, *Beyond the Milky Way: Hallucinatory Imagery of the Tukano Indians* (Los Angeles, CA, 1978), p. 11.

27   Joanne Pillsbury, Timothy F. Potts and Kim N. Richter, *Golden Kingdoms: Luxury Arts in the Ancient Americas* (Los Angeles, CA, 2017), p. 253.

28 Hope B. Werness et al., *The Continuum Encyclopedia of Animal Symbolism in Art* (New York, 2004), p. 290.

3 TURTLES, CULTURE AND COMMUNITY

1 Sarah Allan, *The Shape of the Turtle: Myth, Art, and Cosmos in Early China* (Albany, NY, 1991), pp. 103–4.

2 Karen Bassie-Sweet, *Maya Sacred Geography and the Creator Deities* (Norman, OK, 2008), p. 63.

3 Mark Zender, 'Teasing the Turtle from Its Shell: AHK and MAHK in Maya Writing', *The PARI Journal*, VI/3 (2005), p. 9.

4 Zender, 'Teasing the Turtle', p. 9.

5 Merideth Paxton, *The Cosmos of the Yucatec Maya: Cycles and Steps from the Madrid Codex* (Albuquerque, NM, 2001), p. 85.

6 Robert J. Sharer and Loa P. Traxler, *The Ancient Maya* (Stanford, CA, 2006), p. 118.

7 Hilary N. Weaver, *Social Issues in Contemporary Native America: Reflections from Turtle Island* (New York, 2014), p. 1.

8 Bill Grantham, *Creation Myths and Legends of the Creek Indians* (Gainesville, FL, 2002), pp. 244–5.

9 Ibid., p. 245.

10 Lorelei A. Lambert, *Keepers of the Central Fire: Issues in Ecology for Indigenous Peoples* (Sudbury, MA, 1998), p. 28.

11 Rocío Álvarez-Varas et al., 'Conservation Research Needs of Easter Island (Rapa Nui) Marine Turtles', *Chelonian Conservation and Biology*, XIV/2 (2015), pp. 184–92.

12 Dean Miller, *Animals and Animal Symbols in World Culture* (New York, 2014), p. 138.

13 Margaret Mead, *Letters from the Field, 1925–1975* (New York, 1977), pp. 30–31.

14 Davianna Pōmaika'I McGregor, *Nā Kuàāina: Living Hawaiian Culture* (Honolulu, HI, 2007), p. 75.

15 Philip Hayward, 'Japan: The "Mermaidisation" of the Ningyo and Related Folkloric Figures', in *Scaled for Success: The Internationalisation of the Mermaid*, ed. Philip Hayward (East Barnet, 2018), p. 65.

16 Kay Almere Read and Jason J. Gonzalez, *Mesoamerican Mythology: A Guide to the Gods, Heroes, Rituals, and Beliefs of Mexico and Central America* (Oxford, 2000), p. 251.

17 Sarah Keith and Sung-Ae Lee, 'Legend of the Blue Sea: Mermaids in South Korean Folklore and Popular Culture', in *Scaled for Success*, ed. Hayward, p. 73.

18 Lucy Andrew, 'Secret Missions with Souped-up Sonar', ABC, www.abc.net.au, 4 February 2004.

19 Jeffrey E. Lovich et al., 'Where Have All the Turtles Gone, and Why Does It Matter?', *BioScience*, LXVIII/10.1 (2018), https://doi.org/10.1093/biosci/biy095, p. 7.

20 Ibid., pp. 3–4.

21 N. J. Robinson et al., 'Epibiotic Diatoms Are Universally Present on All Sea Turtle Species', *PLOS ONE*, XI/6 (2016), www.journals.plos.org, accessed 3 June 2016.

22 Nathan J. Robinson et al., 'Assortative Epibiosis of Leatherback, Olive Ridley and Green Sea Turtles in the Eastern Tropical Pacific', *Journal of the Marine Biological Association of the United Kingdom*, XCVII/ 6 (2017), p. 1233.

23 Nathan Jack Robinson, 'Sea Turtle "Hitchhikers" Could Play an Important Role in Conservation', *The Conversation*, www.theconversation.com, 15 July 2016.

4 TURTLES, TRADE AND TECHNOLOGY

1 Alessandro Delli Paoli Carini et al., 'Antibiotic Resistant Bacterial Isolates from Captive Green Turtles and In Vitro Sensitivity to Bacteriophages', *International Journal of Microbiology*, III (2017), pp. 1–8.

2 David J. Duffy et al., 'Sea Turtle Fibropapilloma Tumors Share Genomic Drivers and Therapeutic Vulnerabilities with Human Cancers', *Communications Biology*, 1/63 (2018), https://doi.org/10.1038/s42003-018-0059-x.

3 Jessica Alice Farrell, 'Could Human Cancer Treatments Be the Key to Saving Sea Turtles from a Disfiguring Tumor Disease?', www.theconversation.com, 11 July 2018.

4   Duffy, 'Sea Turtle Tumors'.
5   Y. Haridy et al., 'Triassic Cancer – Osteosarcoma in a 240-Million-year-old Stem-turtle', *JAMA Oncology*, V/3, https://jamanetwork.com, 7 February 2019.
6   Yasemin Saplakoglu, '"Oldest" Case of Bone Cancer Is Diagnosed in a 240-million-year-old Shell-less Turtle', www.livescience.com, 7 February 2019.
7   Jane J. Lee, 'First "Glowing" Sea Turtle Found', www.nationalgeographic.com, 28 September 2015.
8   Archie Carr, *Handbook for Turtles* (Ithaca, NY, 1952).
9   Callum Roberts, *The Unnatural History of the Sea* (Washington, DC, 2007), p. 66.
10 'Turtles', *Daily Alta California*, II/215, 14 July 1851.
11 Leslie Nemo, 'Why Gold Rush Miners Imported Sea Turtles', www.atlasobscura.com, 13 February 2018.
12 Amelia Simmons, *American Cookery*, 2nd edn (Albany, NY, 1796), facsimile, with introduction by Karen Hess (1996).
13 Keith W. F. Stavely and Kathleen Fitzgerald, *United Tastes: The Making of the First American Cookbook* (Amherst, MA, 2017), p. 194.
14 B. W. Higman, 'Cookbooks and Caribbean Cultural Identity: An English-language Hors d'Oeuvre', *NWIG: New West Indian Guide / Nieuwe West-Indische Gids*, LXXII/1/2 (1998), p. 75.
15 Suzy Freeman-Greene, 'Eating Turtle: Changing Narratives of the Normal', *Griffith Review*, 63 (2019), p. 91.
16 Ibid., p. 91.
17 Jeffrey E. Lovich and Katsuya Yamamoto, 'Measuring the Impact of Invasive Species on Popular Culture: A Case Study Based on Toy Turtles from Japan', *Humans and Nature*, XXVII (2016), pp. 1–11.
18 'Spanish Police Shut Down What May Be Europe's Biggest Illegal Turtle Farm', www.bloomberg.com, 23 August 2018.
19 Nairana Santos et al., 'Review: Cadmium in Tissues of Green Turtles (*Chelonia mydas*): A Global Perspective for Marine Biota', *Science of the Total Environment*, 637–8 (2018), pp. 389–97.
20 Thomas Hinton and David Scott, 'Radioecological Techniques for Herpetology, with an Emphasis on Freshwater Turtles', in *Life*

History and Ecology of the Slider Turtle*, ed. J. W. Gibbons (Washington, DC, 1990), p. 283.

21 Ibid., p. 269.

22 Thomas Hainschwang and Laurence Leggi, 'Characterization of Tortoise Shell and Its Imitations', *Gems and Gemology*, XLII/1 (Spring 2006), pp. 35–52.

23 Himanshu Prabha Ray, *The Archaeology of Seafaring in Ancient South Asia* (Cambridge and New York, 2003), p. 38.

24 Christophe Pourny, *The Furniture Bible: Everything You Need to Know to Identify, Restore, and Care for Furniture* (New York, 2014), p. 8.

25 Gary Strieker, 'Tortoiseshell Ban Threatens Japanese Tradition', www.cnn.com, 10 April 2001.

26 Peta Bee, 'Anti-dopers Can't Hope to Solve This Chinese Puzzle', www.theguardian.com, 26 April 2004.

27 'Cape Cod Turtles "Flying" South for the Winter', www. southcoasttoday.com, 12 December 2018.

28 Sŏng-do Cho, Joo-sik Kim and Chin-sul Chŏng, *Admiral Yi Sun-Sin: A National Hero of Korea* (Seoul, 2005), p. 62.

29 Choi Wan Gee, *The Traditional Ships of Korea*, trans. Lee Jean Young (Seoul, 2006), p. 94.

30 Ibid.

31 Letter from George Washington to Thomas Jefferson, 26 September 1785, www.founders.archives.gov, 13 June 2018. (Original source: W. W. Abbot, ed., *The Papers of George Washington, Confederation Series* (Charlottesville, VA, 1994), vol. III, pp. 279–83.)

32 'The Gallipoli Turtle', www.armymuseum.co.nz, accessed 24 January 2019.

5 MODERN ART AND LITERATURE

1 Carl Safina, *Voyage of the Turtle: In Pursuit of the Earth's Last Dinosaur* (New York, 2006), p. 1.

2 Ogden Nash, 'Autres Betes, Autres Moeurs II', 1931, reprinted in the *New Yorker*, 5 August 2002, www.newyorker.com, accessed 28 November 2019.

3 Ogden Nash, 'Carnival of the Animals', 7 January 1950, *New Yorker*, www.thenewyorker.com, accessed 28 November 2019.
4 Kay Ryan, *Flamingo Watching* (London, 1994).
5 Randy Malamud, 'Poetic Animals and Animal Souls', *Society and Animals*, vi/3 (1998), pp. 263–77.
6 Sylvester Bickford, 'The Cuban Context of *The Old Man and the Sea*', in *The Cambridge Companion to Hemingway*, ed. Scott Donaldson (Cambridge, 1996), p. 245.
7 Gary Snyder, *Turtle Island* (New York, 1974).
8 Terry Pratchett, *The Colour of Magic* (Sydney, 1983).
9 Terry Pratchett, *The Light Fantastic* (Sydney, 1986), p. 177.
10 Philip Nel, *Dr Seuss: An American Icon* (New York, 2004).
11 Jennie Rothenberg Gritz, 'When Dr Seuss Took on Adolf Hitler', www.theatlantic.com, 15 January 2013.
12 Dr Seuss, *Yertle the Turtle and Other Stories* (New York, 1957).
13 Saul Andreetti, 'The Inner Compass: Myth, Emotion and Trauma in *The Neverending Story*', in *Myth and Emotions*, ed. José Manuel Losada and Antonella Lipscomb (Newcastle upon Tyne, 2017), pp. 157–66.
14 Lauren Duca, 'The Hand-made Magic of *The NeverEnding Story*', www.huffingtonpost.com, 7 December 2017.
15 John J. Muth, *The Three Questions* (New York, 2002).
16 Lewis Carroll, *Alice's Adventures in Wonderland*, illus. John Tenniel (London, 1867), p. 139.
17 Herbert Friedmann, 'Footnotes to the Painted Page: The Iconography of an Altarpiece by Botticini', *Metropolitan Museum of Art Bulletin*, xxviii/1 (1969), p. 12.
18 Mark G. Boyer, *An Abecedarian of Animal Spirit Guides: Spiritual Growth through Reflections on Creatures* (Eugene, or, 2016), p. 182.
19 Jack Flam, *Matisse and Picasso: The Story of Their Rivalry and Friendship* (New York, 2003), pp. 45–65.
20 John Elderfield, 'Moving Aphrodite: On the Genesis of *Bathers with a Turtle* by Henri Matisse', *Bulletin (Saint Louis Art Museum)*, xxii/3 (1998), pp. 20–49.
21 Roland Penrose, *Picasso, His Life and Work* (London, 1958).

22 Oral history interview with Joseph Pulitzer, 11 January 1978, Archives of American Art, Smithsonian Institution, www.aaa.si. edu, accessed 12 December 2018.

23 Jonathan Jones, 'Emil Nolde Review – A Seething Visionary Twisted by Antisemitism', www.theguardian.com, 13 February 2018.

24 'The Tortoise Trainer', https://en.peramuzesi.org.tr, accessed 10 December 2018.

25 Salvador Dalí, *The Secret Life of Salvador Dalí* (New York, 1942).

26 Richard R. Brettell, Paul Hayes Tucker and Natalie H. Lee, *The Robert Lehman Collection at the Metropolitan Museum of Art*, vol. III: *Nineteenth- and Twentieth-century Paintings* (Princeton, NJ, 2009), p. 290.

6 TURTLE POWER: POPULAR CULTURE AND TURTLES

1 Christopher Blomquist, *Green Sea Turtles* (New York, 2005), p. 5.

2 Peter Young, *Tortoise* (London, 2013).

3 Ibid.

4 Brian Jay Jones, *Jim Henson: The Biography* (New York, 2013), p. 211.

5 Chris York and Rafiel York, eds, *Comic Books and the Cold War, 1946–1962: Essays on Graphic Treatment of Communism, the Code and Social Concerns* (Jefferson, NC, 2012), p. 61.

6 Sean Rhoads and Brooke McCorkle, *Japan's Green Monsters. Environmental Commentary in Kaiju Cinema* (Jefferson, NC, 2018), p. 90.

7 Andrew Farago, *Teenage Mutant Ninja Turtles: The Ultimate Visual History* (San Rafael, CA, 2014), p. 64.

8 Kenneth D. Rose, *One Nation Underground: The Fallout Shelter in American Culture* (New York, 2001), p. 128.

9 Tracy C. Davis, *Stages of Emergency: Cold War Nuclear Civil Defense* (Durham, NC, 2007), p. 108.

10 Ibid.

1   Jeffrey E. Lovich et al., 'Where Have All the Turtles Gone,
    and Why Does It Matter?', *BioScience*, LXVIII/10.1 (2018),
    https://doi.org/10.1093/biosci/biy095, accessed
    27 November 2019.
2   David A. Fennell, *Ecotourism* (London, 2014), p. 19.
3   Celmara Pocock, 'Turtle Riding on the Great Barrier Reef ',
    Society and Animals, XIV/2 (2006), pp. 129–46.
4   Ibid.
5   Don Moll and Edward O. Moll, *The Ecology, Exploitation and
    Conservation of River Turtles* (Oxford, 2004), p. 226.
6   Ibid.
7   Duncan Campbell, 'Close but No Cigar: How America Failed
    to Kill Fidel Castro', www.theguardian.com, 1 November 2016.
8   Yury Fedotov and John E. Scanlon, 'Wildlife Crime Ranks among
    Trafficking in Drugs, Arms and Humans', www.theguardian.com,
    27 September 2013.
9   Ibid.
10 Paul Maguire, personal telephone communication,
    16 October 2014.
11 Janine E. Robinson et. al., 'Captive Reptile Mortality Rates
    in the Home and Implications for the Wildlife Trade', *PLOS ONE*,
    X/11 (2015), https://doi.org/10.1371/journal.pone.0157519, ac-
    cessed 27 November 2019.
12 Paul Maguire, personal telephone communication.
13 Peter Aldhous, 'Turtle Conservationist Murdered in Costa Rica',
    www.newscientist.com, 3 June 2018.
14 Jack Barry, 'Costa Rican Drug Addicts Are Killing Turtles and
    Conservationists', www.vice.com, 19 June 2013.
15 Ian Burrell, 'Turtle Conservationist Shot Dead "by Poachers"
    on Costa Rica Beach', www.independent.co.uk, 13 June 2013.
16 'Poachers Smash Police Car, Escape with Nesting Turtle',
    caymannewsservice.com, 20 July 2018.
17 'Battle against Turtle Poaching Continues', caymannewsservice.
    com, 23 July 2018.

18   Tanya Wyatt, 'Uncovering the Significance of and Motivation for Wildlife Trafficking', in *Routledge International Handbook of Green Criminology*, ed. Nigel South and Avi Brisman (New York, 2013), p. 302.
19   Christopher Vandome, 'The Illegal Wildlife Trade Conference Highlights the Economic Benefits of Conservation', www.independent.co.uk, 11 October 2018.
20   W. B. Karesh et al., 'Wildlife Trade and Global Disease Emergence', *Emerging Infectious Diseases*, xi/7 (July 2005), pp. 1000–1002.
21   Katherine Hobson, 'Illegal Trade in Tiny Pet Turtles Keeps Spreading Salmonella', www.npr.org, 23 December 2015.
22   'Pet Turtle Sales Banned by the FDA', www.nytimes.com, 21 May 1975.
23   Ibid.
24   Denise Grady, 'Tiny Pet Turtles Return: Salmonella Does, Too', www.nytimes.com, 15 March 2005.
25   'Weekly Almanac', *Jet Magazine*, LV/1 (21 September 1978), p. 19.
26   Lovich et al., 'Where Have All the Turtles Gone?'

Select Bibliography

Carr, Archie, *The Sea Turtle: So Excellent a Fishe* (Garden City, NY, 1986)

Ernst, Carl H., and Jeffrey E. Lovich, *Turtles of the United States and Canada*, 2nd edn (Baltimore, MD, 2009)

Franklin, Carl J., *Turtles: An Extraordinary Natural History 245 Million Years in the Making* (McGregor, MN, 2007)

Gibbons, Whitfield J., Judy Greene and Cris Hagen, *Turtles: The Animal Answer Guide* (Baltimore, MD, 2009)

Lovich, Jeffrey E., et al., 'Where Have All the Turtles Gone, and Why Does It Matter?', *BioScience*, LXVIII/10.1 (2018), pp. 771–81

Lutz, Peter L., and John A. Musick, eds, *The Biology of Sea Turtles* (Boca Raton, FL, 1997)

Orenstein, Ronald, *Turtles, Tortoises and Terrapins: Survivors in Armor* (Buffalo, NY, 2001)

Pritchard, Peter C. H., *Encyclopedia of Turtles* (Neptune City, NJ, 1980)

Spotila, James R., *Sea Turtles: A Complete Guide to Their Biology, Behavior, and Conservation* (Baltimore, MD, 2004)

Witherington, Blair E., *Sea Turtles: An Extraordinary Natural History of Some Uncommon Turtles* (St Paul, MN, 2006)

Associations and Websites

THE ARCHIE CARR CENTRE FOR SEA TURTLE RESEARCH
https://accstr.ufl.edu

ONLINE SEA TURTLE BIBLIOGRAPHY
http://st.cits.fcla.edu/st.jsp

BRITISH CHELONIA GROUP
www.britishcheloniagroup.org.uk

CALIFORNIA TURTLE & TORTOISE CLUB
https://tortoise.org

CHELONIAN RESEARCH FOUNDATION
www.chelonian.org

THE LEATHERBACK TRUST
https://leatherback.org

SEA TURTLE CONSERVANCY
https://conserveturtles.org

SEA TURTLE FOUNDATION
www.seaturtlefoundation.org

SEATURTLE.ORG
www.seaturtle.org

SEE TURTLES.ORG
www.seeturtles.org

THE TURTLE CONSERVANCY
www.turtleconservancy.org

THE TURTLE SURVIVAL ALLIANCE
https://turtlesurvival.org

WIDER CARIBBEAN SEA TURTLE CONSERVATION NETWORK
www.widecast.org

Acknowledgements

In the journey of writing *Turtle*, many people have provided generous support and guidance.

My students from Macquarie University have contributed with wonderful enthusiasm. My thanks go to Emma Bolton, Elise Cannon, Katherine Shead and Laura Skillicorn, particularly for giving me Tertullian, the book's plush turtle mascot. I am most grateful for further turtle mascots provided by Lea Beness and Tom Hillard. I thank my research assistant, Paul Statheos, for his diligence and support, and Rebecca Kuper for her assistance. I would also like to thank Penny Edwell and Macquarie's Museum of Ancient Cultures.

My thanks go to the Nicholson Museum at the University of Sydney, and my friends, colleagues and former students at Sydney, especially Emma Barlow, Marija Rodriguez, Christopher Malone and Zachary Phillips. I am grateful for the assistance of Michelle Momdjian. I'd like to acknowledge the kind assistance of Wayne Horowitz and Tzvi Abusch.

Many turtle experts and organizations generously lent their time and expertise to this endeavour. My thanks go to Rod Kennett, Jeffrey Lovich and Whit Gibbons. I'd also like to thank Johanna Karam and the Sea Turtle Foundation, as well as Erin Wyatt and Seaworld. Many grateful thanks also to Michael Leaman, Jonathan Burt, Alex Ciobanu, Harry Gilonis and Amy Salter at Reaktion Books, for their encouragement and help. Of course, all mistakes are my own.

I very much appreciate the assistance of the Maui Ocean Centre, with special thanks to Amy Fonarow and Tommy Cutt. My thanks to

George J. Craig, of Green Island. My friends and former colleagues at Taronga Zoo have been greatly helpful.

Finally, I'd like to acknowledge the memory of Taronga Zoo's Loz Hush. Loz loved all reptiles (and turtles!), and her commitment to conservation provided wonderful inspiration for everyone who had the privilege of knowing her.

Photo Acknowledgements

The author and publishers wish to express their thanks to the following sources of illustrative material and/or permission to reproduce it. Some locations are also supplied here for reasons of brevity.

© The Andy Warhol Foundation for the Visual Arts, Inc/ARS Copyright Agency, 2020: p. 133; photo Jose Aragones/Pexels: p. 89; Australian National Maritime Museum, Sydney: p. 160; from *Birds and All Nature*, v/2 (2 February 1899): p. 65; The British Museum, London: pp. 8, 47, 58, 119; photo Adrijana Bundalo/Pexels: p. 9; from Lewis Carroll, *Alice's Adventures in Wonderland* (London, 1866): p. 126; from Mark Catesby, *The Natural History of Carolina, Florida and the Bahama Islands*, vol. II (London, 1743): p. 88; Château Ramezay – Historic Site and Museum of Montréal, QC/photo Daderot: p. 60 (top); photo Coast Guard Cutter *Lawrence Lawson*/U.S. Department of Defense: p. 84; Cooper Hewitt, Smithsonian Design Museum, New York (Open Access): p. 93; photo courtesy George J. Craig/Marineland Melanesia: p. 74; photo Moe Faroy/Pexels: p. 164; Fernbank Museum of Natural History, Atlanta, GA/photo Daderot: p. 62; from Conrad Gessner, *Nomenclator aquatilium animantium: icones animalium in mari et dulcibus aquis degentium* (Zürich, 1560): p. 20; photo Golden Harvest/Kobal/Shutterstock: p. 149; from Ernst Haeckel, *Kunstformen der Natur* (Leipzig and Vienna, 1904), photo courtesy Library of Congress, Washington, DC: p. 17; from Joel Chandler Harris, *Uncle Remus, His Songs and His Sayings: The Folk-lore of the Old Plantation* (New York, 1881): p. 121; photo courtesy Malinda Hayward: p. 71 (right); from Austen Henry Layard, ed., *A Second Series of the Monuments of Nineveh* (London, 1853): p. 46; Library of Congress, Prints

Index

Alice's Adventures in Wonderland 125–6, *126*
Amin, Idi 166–7
American Turtle 108–9, *109*
Aphrodite 55–6, *57*, 127
artificial light 156–7, *157*

basking 37–8, *38*
Bermuda 87, 112
Bey, Osman Hamdi, *The Tortoise Trainer* 127, *131*
Bible, the 54–5

camouflage 24, *24*, 79, 85
Capone, Al 105–7
Carr, Archie 29, 87
China 22, 49–51, 94, 100
climate change and sex determination 12, 156–7
coinage 54, 55, *55*, 56
comics 145–151
communication 30, 39–40, 80, 166–7
Columbus, Christopher 86–7
Cretaceous period 16, 41
Cuvier, Georges 17

Dalí, Salvador 129–30
definition 8
diving 7, 15, 35–6, 67, 78
Dr Seuss
    Yertle the Turtle 122–3
Duck and Cover
    Bert the Turtle 94, 152–4, 153

ecotourism 155, 157–60
eggs 28–9, 33–5, 35, 48, 71, 81, 87, 95, 133–4, 157–9, 162–4, *162*
Egypt 52–4

Finding Nemo 151–2
fossils 15–22, *42*, 84
Franklin the Turtle 135, 139, *139*
flippers 24, 26, 27, 55, 86, *117*, 143

Galápagos tortoise 30, 88–90, *89*
Gallipoli 110–11
Gamera 146–8, *147*
Geobukseon, the 'Turtle Ship' 107–8

Gessner, Conrad 21
    woodcut turtle drawing *20*
Godward, John William,
    The Quiet Pet 114
gold rush 88–90
Greek myth 55–8
green turtle 7, *24*, 33, 73, 82, 87,
    96, 97

Haeckel, Ernst 18
    Kunstformen der Natur 17
Hawaiian myth 72–3
Hemingway, Ernest 116–17
Hitler, Adolf 122, 128
Hokusai, Katsushika, turtle
    drawing *75*

illegal wildlife trade 160–66
Illinois Humane Society,
    the 106–7, 112

Japan 51–2, 74–6, 94, 99,
    147–8
Jamaica 87

Korea 77, 104, 107–8
Kung Fu Panda 151, *152*

Laessle, Albert 132–3
leatherback turtles 26, 33, 35,
    36–7, 79
life cycle 27–32
Looney Tunes
    Cecil the Turtle and Bugs
    Bunny 135, 138, 141–2
longevity 31–3, 63, 151

Matisse, Henri, *Bathers with a
    Turtle* 127–8, 130
medicine 44, 60, 68, 81–6, 94,
    100–102, 111, 161
Melanesian culture 73–74
Mesoamerica 59–61, 65–6
Mesopotamia 44–8
Monteiro, Vicente do Rego 130
Mora Sandoval, Jairo 162–3, *163*
Muppets, The
    'Turtle Soup' 144–5
music 43, 58–61, 73, 77, 80, 129,
    143, 149

nesting 33–5, *34*, *35*, 39–40, 72,
    78, 156–9, 162, 164
Neverending Story, The 123–4
Ninurta and the Turtle (myth) 46–7
Nolde, Emil, *Swimming Turtle* 129
northern snake-necked turtle
    27–9

olive ridley turtle 37, 79
omens 44–5, 49, 60, 100, *102*

Pappochelys rosinae 20, *21*
Pausanias 55, 58
pets 10, 32, 93, 94, *114*, 127,
    160–62, 165–6
Picasso, Pablo 127
pirates 87–8
Plutarch 39, 56
poetry 113–16
Porpora, Paolo, *Turtle and Crab
    115*
Proganochelys quenstedti 19

red-eared slider turtles 93–4, 94,
    151, 160
rock art 8, 10, 77
'reptiles' 14, 16–19

Samaon myth 71–2
sea exploration 86–90
Sesame Street
    Sheldon 'Shelley' Turtle 142–4
sexual behaviour 29–31
shell 10, 23–25
Snyder, Gary 113, 117–18
Snyders, Frans, *Fable of the Hare
    and the Tortoise* 141
space exploration 103–4

Teenage Mutant Ninja Turtles
    10–11, 27, 148–51, *149*
Thoreau, Henry David 14, 113
Three Questions, The 124–5
tortoiseshell 58–9, 98–102, 113
Triassic period 16, 21, 84
Turtle and the Hare (fable) 104,
    122, 138–42, *141*, 168–9
Turtle Diary 116, *118*
turtle racing 104–7
turtle riding 76, 159–60, *160*
turtle soup 144–5, 90–94, *92*, *95*,
    111, 126

Uncle Remus
    Brer Rabbit and Brer
    Tarrypin 120–22, *121*

Warhol, Andy 130, 132
    Turtle 133

wisdom 7, 8, 9, 45–8, 49, 60, 63,
    68, 75–6, 113, 123–5, 151–2
world turtle 63–8, 79–80, 118–20

yoga 69–70, *71*